TWELVE STEPS FOR OVEREATERS

TWELVE STEPS
FOR OVEREATERS

An Interpretation of the Twelve Steps
of Overeaters Anonymous

Elisabeth L.

HazeLDeN®

Hazelden
Center City, Minnesota 55012-0176

ISBN: 0-89486-905-1

Step One: When Willpower Is Not Enough is from the pamphlet *Step One: When Willpower Is Not Enough* by Elisabeth L. © 1982 by Hazelden Foundation. *Step Two: You Are Not Alone* is from the pamphlet *Step Two: You Are Not Alone* by Elisabeth L. © 1982 by Hazelden Foundation. *Step Three: Giving Up the Game* is from the pamphlet *Step Three: Giving Up the Game* by Elisabeth L. © 1982 by Hazelden Foundation. *Step Four: Face to Face with Yourself* is from the pamphlet *Step Four: Face to Face with Yourself* by Elisabeth L. © 1983 by Hazelden Foundation. *Step Five: And the Truth Will Set You Free* is from the pamphlet *Step Five: And the Truth Will Set You Free* by Elisabeth L. © 1983 by Hazelden Foundation. *Step Six: Getting Ready to Let Go* is from the pamphlet *Step Six: Getting Ready to Let Go* by Elisabeth L. © 1983 by Hazelden Foundation. *Step Seven: Let Go and Let God* is from the pamphlet *Let Go and Let God* by Elisabeth L. © 1983 by Hazelden Foundation. *Step Eight: Getting Honest* is from the pamphlet *Step Eight: Getting Honest* by Elisabeth L. © 1983 by Hazelden Foundation. *Step Nine: Building Bridges* is from the pamphlet *Step Nine: Building Bridges* by Elisabeth L. © 1983 by Hazelden Foundation. *Step Ten: Accepting Ourselves* is from the pamphlet *Step Ten: Accepting Ourselves* by Elisabeth L. © 1983 by Hazelden Foundation. *Step Eleven: Centering Ourselves* is from the pamphlet *Step Eleven: Centering Ourselves* by Elisabeth L. © 1983 by Hazelden Foundation. *Step Twelve: Living the Program* is from the pamphlet *Step Twelve: Living the Program* by Elisabeth L. © 1983 by Hazelden Foundation.

CONTENTS

INTRODUCTION

Some of us say we found the program. Others of us say the program found us. Whichever way it happened, those of us who practice the Twelve Steps of Overeaters Anonymous (OA) are very lucky. We have the blueprint for a way of life that can free us from the obsession with food.

Most of us struggled long and hard to control what we ate and to escape the binge/diet trap. We tried all sorts of ways to stop using food to solve emotional problems. We wanted to be rid of the compulsion to overeat, to undereat, to binge and purge. When the diets didn't work, and the exercise programs didn't work, either, and nothing else we tried worked, some of us were ready to admit our powerlessness over food and the unmanageability of our lives.

We felt an emptiness inside that no amount of food could fill. So when we came to the Twelve Step program, we were desperate enough to entertain the idea of a spiritual solution. For me, as for many of you, it was the only way left.

I knew that the Twelve Step program worked for alcoholics. As I began going to OA meetings, I saw those Steps changing the lives of people who had been obsessed with food. I was a compulsive overeater. Maybe the Twelve Steps could work for me.

Like most people with eating disorders, I knew what I should eat. Knowing was not the problem; that was easy. It was the doing that was difficult, if not impossible. One day I would eat twelve hundred calories' worth of food, and the next day I would eat that much plus a half gallon of ice cream. No matter how much I ate, it was never enough.

When I got to the Twelve Step program, I was ready to concede that I was powerless over food. It took considerably longer to accept the fact that I was also powerless over people, places, and things, but in the process of getting to that point, I was slowly discovering a new way of life.

For me, the Steps have been the key to strengthening the spiritual dimension that is available to us all. Even though no amount of food fills my inner emptiness, no amount of willpower prevents me from bingeing. The way I can avoid trying to use food to solve problems food can't solve is by getting in touch with a source of strength beyond myself—a Higher Power.

Our program is a spiritual one, not a diet-and-calories club. Many of us start out thinking that if we could just eat "normally" and maintain an ideal weight, everything would be perfect. Before we get very far along, however, we begin to realize that simply not bingeing is not enough, and ideal weight is not enough, either. Life's challenges are more complex. What we need is a program for living, a positive way of dealing with the ups and downs of everyday reality so that we don't need to escape into harmful dependencies.

For me, the Twelve Steps point the way to a healthy dependency on a Higher Power. I take them over and over again. I have been in the program for more than ten years, and each year gets better. The more thoroughly I practice the principles, the easier it is to cope with whatever comes my way, one day at a time. Amazing changes have taken place in my life. With a Higher Power in charge, I don't have to depend on excess food to see me through. Excess food didn't work. The Higher Power, whom I choose to call God, does.

The beauty of our program is that it gives us freedom of choice. Nothing is mandatory. The Steps are "suggested," not imposed, and each of us who takes the Steps does so in the way that best suits her or him individually. We all have the benefit of other people's experience, and most of us choose to work with a sponsor.

When I embarked on the Steps, it was with the help of my OA group, my sponsor, and "Twelve and Twelve," the book describing the Twelve Steps for Alcoholics Anonymous. As I continue this rewarding journey, I am guided and nourished by the experience, strength, and hope of all of you, as together we do what we cannot do alone. What I have written down in the following pages represents my own interpretation of the Steps, based on the gifts I have received in the meeting rooms and what has come out of my personal experience.

I am very grateful to have found and been found by the Twelve Step program of Overeaters Anonymous. For me, abstinence from compulsive overeating is possible when spiritual growth is my first priority.

Working the Steps is what keeps me on track. Because our program is a spiritual one, there is no limit to the progress we can make. Each day, each year brings new discoveries. It is my hope that each of you who reads this book will find it helpful as you develop and continue your own program of recovery and "become happily and usefully whole."*

---

* *Twelve Steps and Twelve Traditions* (New York: Alcoholics Anonymous World Services, Inc., 1952). Subsequent references to this book, which will appear parenthetically in the text, will use the short title "Twelve and Twelve" and give page numbers.

The Twelve Steps of Alcoholics Anonymous[*]

1. We admitted we were powerless over alcohol—that our lives had become unmanageable.

2. Came to believe that a Power greater than ourselves could restore us to sanity.

3. Made a decision to turn our will and our lives over to the care of God *as we understood Him.*

4. Made a searching and fearless moral inventory of ourselves.

5. Admitted to God, to ourselves, and to another human being the exact nature of our wrongs.

6. Were entirely ready to have God remove all these defects of character.

7. Humbly asked Him to remove our shortcomings.

8. Made a list of all persons we had harmed, and became willing to make amends to them all.

9. Made direct amends to such people wherever possible, except when to do so would injure them or others.

10. Continued to take personal inventory and when we were wrong promptly admitted it.

11. Sought through prayer and meditation to improve our conscious contact with God *as we understood Him,* praying only for knowledge of His will for us and the power to carry that out.

12. Having had a spiritual awakening as the result of these steps, we tried to carry this message to alcoholics, and to practice these principles in all our affairs.

---

[*]The Twelve Steps of AA are taken from *Alcoholics Anonymous,* 3d ed., published by AA World Services, Inc., New York, N.Y., 59-60. Reprinted with permission of AA World Services, Inc. (See editor's note on the copyright page.)

The Twelve Steps of Overeaters Anonymous*

1. We admitted we were powerless over food—that our lives had become unmanageable.
2. Came to believe that a Power greater than ourselves could restore us to sanity.
3. Made a decision to turn our will and our lives over to the care of God *as we understood Him.*
4. Made a searching and fearless moral inventory of ourselves.
5. Admitted to God, to ourselves and to another human being the exact nature of our wrongs.
6. Were entirely ready to have God remove all these defects of character.
7. Humbly asked Him to remove our shortcomings.
8. Made a list of all persons we had harmed, and became willing to make amends to them all.
9. Made direct amends to such people wherever possible, except when to do so would injure them or others.
10. Continued to take personal inventory and when we were wrong promptly admitted it.
11. Sought through prayer and meditation to improve our conscious contact with God *as we understood Him,* praying only for knowledge of His will for us and the power to carry that out.
12. Having had a spiritual awakening as the result of these steps, we tried to carry this message to compulsive overeaters and to practice these principles in all our affairs.

---

*From *Overeaters Anonymous* © 1980 by Overeaters Anonymous, Torrance, Calif., p. 4. Adapted from the Twelve Steps of Alcoholics Anonymous in *Alcoholics Anonymous* 3d ed., published by AA World Services, Inc., New York, N.Y., 59-60. Reprinted with permission of AA World Services, Inc. (See editor's note on the copyright page.)

WHEN WILLPOWER IS NOT ENOUGH

We admitted we were powerless over food—that our lives had become unmanageable.

W hat does it mean to be so powerless over food that you are unable to manage your life? It might mean that you are 150 pounds overweight and in danger of losing your job as well as your health. It might mean that you spend most of your waking hours planning to diet but inevitably you begin to binge again and once more outgrow the clothes in your closet. It might mean that you consume huge quantities of food, then vomit so that you won't gain weight, and live in constant fear that people will find out how crazy you are. It might mean that you spend so much time eating and thinking about food that the rest of your life is in a shambles. It might mean that you hate not only yourself but almost everyone around you.

If you are controlled by an obsession with food, you probably know it at some level, even though you may not be ready to admit it to yourself or anyone else. "Oh yes, I've put on a few pounds, but I can easily lose them if I set my mind to it—just a matter of finding the right diet and sticking to it."

We all tell this to ourselves when food and eating and weight are a problem, and we proceed to look for the perfect diet. Or we try to rearrange our circumstances so that we will be motivated to eat less. Some of the methods may work for a short time, but for the compulsive overeater none of them works very long.

How far do you have to go to hit bottom? Not far for some. Farther for others. The good news is that when we finally admit that the problem is more than we can manage by ourselves, we have a place to go and a program that will lead us out of the mire of compulsive overeating.

The Twelve Steps of Overeaters Anonymous are the same as the Twelve Steps of Alcoholics Anonymous, substituting the word *food* for *alcohol.* OA considers compulsive overeating to be an illness similar to alcoholism or drug addiction, and the Twelve Steps are a proven way to recovery.

Fat is a symptom of our illness. Although it is possible to overeat compulsively and not be fat, many of us come to OA because we don't like the way we look. We have tried to diet over and over, with little or no success. Our lives have become more and more chaotic and unhappy, and we feel that there must be a way out of the mess.

There is.

But in order to begin to get well, we need to admit that we are sick. It may be that you have been denying your problem with food for years. Do you eat alone, when no one can see how much you consume? Do you hide stashes of goodies where only you can find them? Have you ever finished a complete dinner and then headed for the kitchen or the nearest food store to gulp down the equivalent of several more dinners?

To admit that we are powerless over food is difficult for most of us. What our instincts seem to demand is *more* power of every kind, not less. And food — the source of physical nourishment — seems such a good and necessary part of our existence. How can something so basic and so indispensable lead us astray?

There is nothing wrong with food, but there is something wrong with us when we cannot stop eating once we get started. The first Step to the recovery OA promises is to recognize that we are indeed incapable of managing our behavior when it comes to food. Further, we admit that the disorder created by our compulsive overeating has spilled over into other areas of our lives, making them generally unmanageable. How can you manage your life if you don't know when you will be laid low by the next binge?

Gut-Level Acceptance

It is one thing to know intellectually that you have a problem with food. It is quite another to accept at a deep emotional level the fact that you are powerless to control what you eat. For most of us, such gut-level acceptance comes only after repeated failures to prove that we can achieve control over food and be "normal."

Why can't we eat like other people? A snack here and there. A half piece of cake. A few potato chips. Moderation. Surely we can achieve it if we try hard enough. So we try again and again. And each time we eventually fall flat on our faces into a binge.

Recovery begins when we admit defeat and declare bankruptcy. Until we do this, we are not ready for the kind of rigorous honesty that the OA program demands. As long as we deny that we have an illness over which we have no control—no more control than we would have over diabetes or measles—we will not be motivated to maintain abstinence from compulsive overeating and work the Steps. Abstinence is not easy and neither are the Twelve Steps. Yet this is what has proved successful in arresting the illness and providing a basis for a new, satisfying, and productive life.

If you have tried enough other ways to stop overeating compulsively, you may be ready to agree with those of us who have found that there is no easier, softer way. On a gut level, this means submitting to a feeling of helplessness. "I quit; I throw in the towel; I give up. I may have thought up until now that I could do almost anything I really put my mind to, but this has me licked. If it's up to my efforts alone, I can just resign myself to the fact that I will probably weigh 350 pounds and die early." The ego finally bows to the strength of forces beyond its control.

What About Willpower?

Still not convinced that you are powerless over food? OA recommends that you experiment with a little controlled eating of a favorite food. Can you eat a small portion and stop? Can you have one dish of ice cream, put what remains of the carton back in the freezer, and leave it there? Or do you go back and finish what is left of the ice cream and then move on through the refrigerator, perhaps ending up with cold mashed potatoes?

Ah, but tomorrow will be different, right? Tomorrow you will get back on the diet and stick to it. No ice cream at all, just willpower. Some of us are able to stay on a diet for a period of time, but if we are compulsive overeaters we find that those periods get shorter and shorter as the illness progresses. The diet period dwindles to a week, a day, a morning, and then we may find ourselves bingeing around the clock.

Willpower is fine as far as it goes, but for the compulsive overeater it does not go far enough. The obsession we are trying to control is not rational, so it does not come under the sway of rational resolve. As a matter of fact, it is our "self-will run riot" that pushes us on from bite to bite all the way through a binge; so trying to use self-will to control compulsive overeating is like trying to put out a fire with gasoline. The driving force behind our white-knuckled, clenched-teeth "no" can readily shift over and propel the mania to swallow more and more.

Much as we hate to admit it, an honest review of our behavior as compulsive overeaters shows clearly that in spite of the strongest resolve to stop overeating, we continue. Night after night we go to bed gorged and disgusted; we get up the next morning full of undigested food and fresh determination to maintain control; and before the day is over, we have done it again. No amount of willpower can pull us out of the quicksand.

How About Changing the Circumstances?

"If my mother had not overfed me when I was a baby, I would not be programmed to overeat." "If I had someone who loved me enough, I wouldn't need all this extra food." "If I didn't have so many problems and weren't so tense and upset all the time, I could eat less." "If I move to another city, maybe I can lose weight." "If I get another job, or a wife, or a divorce, or more money . . . if . . . if . . . if . . ."

It is tempting to think that we can cure compulsive overeating by changing our environment and altering the circumstances we don't like. We think we could stop eating too much if we could somehow make ourselves happy. Unhappiness causes us to overeat—so we may believe. Actually, it is the other way around. Overeating makes us unhappy, whatever the external circumstances.

Did you think that you would stop overeating when you graduated from high school and got away from that pressure? When you finally found a good job? When you got married? And were you surprised when the same old pattern repeated itself in the new situation? You may not have been very surprised, but you probably sank deeper into despair.

Blaming our misery on the people and situations around us, we frantically try to manipulate them in order to produce the perfect environment. In the process, we often make things worse. And we are still overeating. Suppose you decide it's your boring job that makes you think about food all the time. You find a job that appears to be more interesting. But you still cannot concentrate. You are so controlled by the progressive compulsion that your attention wanders from your new duties, and you live in constant fear of being fired. Or maybe you can cope with the demands of the job, but you binge every night when you get home. So you decide it's your apartment that needs to be changed, or your husband.

Even if it were possible to pinpoint an exact reason for compulsive eating, it might very well be that the circumstance is impossible to change. Then what do you do? Through the OA program, we learn that we often cannot change external conditions, but we can be changed inside.

Powerless over People, Places, and Things

Along with admitting that we are powerless over food, most of us have come to the conclusion that we are powerless over people, places, and things. We have tried to manipulate them to suit our whims but have not succeeded. The effort has made us tense, fearful, frustrated, and often furious. If we admit that we cannot manage even our own lives, then we can stop trying to make everyone and everything else go the way we want. Attempting to do that is like trying to push water uphill. It is a great relief to give up.

When we take Step One, we stop wearing ourselves out with futile efforts. We concede that we are in the grips of forces beyond our control—first of all an obsession with food and secondly the vicissitudes of life. Events will take their course, the people around us will demand their rights to behave as individuals. What others do may not be what we would advise.

Letting go is what frees us in the long run, but it is often a very hard thing to do. Some of us need to be beaten down pretty far before we are willing to relax our useless mental and emotional efforts to control external circumstances. Step One is often not taken until the compulsive overeater has been devastated over and over again, not only by food but by life itself.

Powerless Every Day

Most of us find that we do not take Step One once and for all. It is something we do repeatedly, often daily. Since denial and self-deception are a part of the illness, we can easily forget that we are compulsive overeaters. This is extremely dangerous.

We don't like the idea of being different from other people. Why shouldn't we be able to eat everything? Well-meaning family and friends can contribute to the self-deception. "It won't hurt you to have one little piece of birthday cake." "You're not overweight; how can you be a compulsive overeater?" "You've been doing so well, you deserve a reward." "Life is too short to deny yourself pleasure."

Life will be even shorter if we kill ourselves with food, and there is little pleasure in the aftereffects of a binge. A compulsive overeater *is* different: he or she is always one bite away from a binge. This is what we need to remember every day.

How we got this way is irrelevant. We are not "bad" people. We are addicted to overeating, especially certain foods, as an alcoholic is addicted to alcohol. We cannot eat spontaneously, on impulse, because once we get started we don't know when we will be able to stop. There is no need to judge ourselves or feel guilty—this is a disease, just as alcoholism and diabetes are diseases.

Similarly, there is no cure for compulsive overeating. It is our experience at OA that no real compulsive overeater ever becomes a normal eater. Those of us who have tried going back to "normal eating" have sooner or later found out through harsh experience that we are still one bite away from a binge. Without the control that comes through the OA program, we are lost.

Paradoxically, the control we gain through the program is given to us when we stop *trying* to manage the food obsession and our lives, and let go of both. Through our weakness comes strength. It is our experience that as long as we think we can do it ourselves by willpower, we continue to fail. Every day.

How many days have you gotten up in the morning full of determination to make this a perfect diet day? How many times have you succeeded? If you are like most of us, without outside help the successful diet days become fewer and fewer and the binges get worse.

So why do we fight taking the first Step of admitting that the situation is beyond our control? Most of us are brought up to think that we should be able to handle our problems and manage our lives independently. Not to be able to do this is to be weak. To say we are powerless over anything goes against all of our conditioning. Besides, giving up control requires giving up the idea of doing things our way. "My way" as a compulsive overeater usually means discovering some secret formula that will enable me to eat what I want, as much as I want, and still lose weight.

Every day, we compulsive overeaters need to remember that our old ways did not work and that we are powerless over food, our appetites, and the habit of overeating.

Isn't There Another Way?

Is there something besides abstinence and the Twelve Steps that you think might work for you? An exercise club? Hypnosis? Eating one meal a day? Fasting? A new diet? If you still think there has to be an easier, softer way, then you probably are not ready to take the Steps or willing to live without your favorite binge foods.

Most of us come to Overeaters Anonymous when all else has failed. For someone who uses excess food to ease tension and dull the pain of living, the idea of abstinence is frightening. A specified number of planned meals (usually three) per day with nothing in between and no binge foods may seem impossible. Probably none of us would be willing to consider abstinence if it were not for the fact that everything else we tried sooner or later failed to solve our eating problem. When we have exhausted all other methods of controlling compulsive overeating, we become desperate enough to concede defeat.

Some of us are able to identify with the stories we hear from compulsive overeaters whose disease has progressed further than our own. A sudden flash of insight may show us where we are headed if our own illness is not arrested. We may recognize patterns in our own behavior similar to those described as early stages in someone else's disease. "There but for the grace of God go I." You may be only ten pounds overweight, or not overweight at all, and still be powerless to control the compulsion to overeat. Sneak eating, a preoccupation with food, periodic binges followed by remorse—these are the signs of a problem that will, if untreated, inevitably get worse.

Slow Destruction

"Okay," you say. "I do eat too much. I have a closet full of clothes in just about every size, and almost everything is too small. But I'm not hurting anyone except myself. If I want to eat my way to an early grave, that's my business. There are many worse things I could be doing." True enough. There are faster ways of killing yourself.

And what about the effects of your overeating on the people around you? What kind of a mood are you in when you have been bingeing for several hours and a child asks for help with homework? What do you say to your boyfriend when he asks you to an impromptu dinner and you have just eaten a large box of cookies? How many times have you picked a fight with your spouse because you were disgusted with yourself? Does she or he want a divorce because all you do at night is eat and watch television?

Are you living your life the way you want to live it? Or is the compulsion to overeat gradually destroying you emotionally and spiritually, as well as physically? How much energy and enthusiasm do you have? For a compulsive overeater who continues to overeat, the answer to this last question is usually "less and less."

Drunk on Food

Do you "need" extra food the way an alcoholic "needs" a drink? Between meals or right after eating a complete dinner, do you crave something more? Is the craving uncontrollable? Does the desire for more drive you to keep eating long after your body's legitimate need for nourishment has been taken care of?

Though it may sound strange, it is possible to be drunk on too much food. Compulsive overeaters attest to passing out during binges, especially when eating large quantities of refined sugar. Getting drunk on food produces a high, followed by a stupor, followed by a hangover. After a binge, sleep is apt to be disturbed. Indigestion, sweating, and a racing mind are common aftereffects. You wake up the next morning feeling as though you've been hit over the head, barely able to get out of bed and drag through the day.

While bingeing, you are out of touch with reality and the rest of the world. After bingeing, you do not have much to give to other people, to your work, or even to some sort of activity that might normally be fun. Overeating saps energy, to say nothing of ruining your disposition. You do and say crazy things that you don't really mean. A compulsive overeater can get drunk on food night after night, day after day.

Like the alcoholic, the overeater gets caught up in a futile quest for satisfaction. Despite consuming more and more, he or she never achieves that magic satiety. No matter how much food is eaten, repletion continues to elude the seeker. It is always in the next bite.

A Life-Giving Program

To anyone who has experienced the chaos and confusion that go along with compulsive overeating, the ability to have three meals a day—period—is a miraculous change. Binges take time and energy. There is the time and attention spent thinking about what and when and how much one will or will not eat. There is the time spent procuring the food and consuming it. And then there is the time spent recovering from the binge. As this activity increases, it crowds out other interests and concerns. Life can eventually become a constant round of eating and remorse, with hardly any time or energy left for anything else.

Taking Step One is the beginning of a new life. Followed honestly, the OA program promises faith and enthusiasm in place of despair— a transformation that is happening to people every day. You can go to meetings all over the country and find examples of changed lives—changed inside as well as outside. The program works if we work it. Step by Step we grow when we are willing first to acknowledge our need for help and then to be open to new ways of thinking and acting. There are no failures with the program, only slow successes.

Admitting that we are powerless makes us ready to change. Our attitude turns from defiance and denial to surrender. "Yes, I am a compulsive overeater. I am powerless over food and my life has become unmanageable." We stop fighting the disease and the fact that we have it. This attitude of surrender is a prerequisite to recovery. According to the Big Book* of Alcoholics Anonymous, pride and self-centered fear are our worst enemies. The ego must surrender if we are to get well.

Surrender will grow and bear fruit as we continue through the Twelve Steps. By means of abstinence, we stop using excess food to try to solve or avoid the problems of life. Slowly but surely, confusion is replaced by order and inner peace. Where before we were full of fear, we become confident and productive. Out of weakness and the admission of utter defeat comes strength.

---

* *Alcoholics Anonymous*, 3rd ed. (New York: A.A. World Services, Inc., 1976) will be called the "Big Book" in subsequent references, and page numbers will be given.

Honesty

A program that requires rigorous honesty sounds forbidding. Probably no one would be willing to undertake abstinence and the Twelve Steps except as a last resort—as the only way to be free of the obsession with food and eating.

Honesty *is* the foundation of recovery. We begin to get honest with ourselves when we admit that we have a problem with food. How many of us blame obesity on a faulty metabolism or glands? "I don't know why I can't lose weight. I hardly eat anything." Anything that anybody *sees* us eat, that is.

If you are a closet eater, you have lots of company. Bingeing in private is part of the disease. If no one sees us eat, it doesn't count—right? We cheat on our diets, and we may be cheating in other areas of life, too. Certainly, we are cheating ourselves out of health and happiness, to say nothing of self-respect and peace of mind.

Some of us can remember sneak eating as children and denying what we had done when confronted with the evidence. We may have blamed the disappearance of the food on someone else, perhaps the dog if no other person was around.

We must get honest about the fact that we are compulsive overeaters. We don't like to admit weakness, especially not to ourselves. It's hard to face the truth, and running away from it can be a conditioned response. How often do you try to escape painful or boring situations by having something to eat? Some of us have used alcohol and drugs along with excess food to try to dull the inevitable pain of living.

In the long run, being dishonest and trying to escape hurts more than facing the truth. The more we avoid reality, the more fearful we become. Pushing down a hurt with a mountain of food does not cure the hurt or make it go away. Whatever we use to drug ourselves, we end up with an additional problem—the harmful effects of abuse.

Large quantities of unnecessary calories can produce a sedating effect for a while, both physically and emotionally. But an honest appraisal will reveal the harm that is being done to body, emotions, and spirit. It's hard to think straight during or after a binge.

The beauty of the Twelve Step program is that it provides a support system to help us get honest. We learn honesty from one another. It's a lot easier to face up to compulsive overeating in a group of people who are doing the same thing and who are sharing their experience, strength, and hope. Before coming to the program, many of us felt that we were the only people in the world who did such crazy things with food, and our isolation produced more suffering.

Honesty, which is the very heart of Step One, is also the basis of the other eleven Steps. We can't work this program and delude ourselves for very long. Now don't panic. The truth about ourselves comes to us in gradual stages, as we become ready to accept it. We don't have to face it all at once, nor could we. Each of us has an individual pattern of inner growth, which unfolds as we go along.

It hurts to face the truth instead of escaping into food, but sometimes we have to hurt in order to get well. In the long run, it is the painful truth that frees us from compulsion.

The Turning Point

Rather than face our powerlessness over persons, places, situations, and life in general, we reached for a prop, something we thought would give us power or something that made us feel powerful temporarily—or at least less powerless. Then we became dependent on the prop—alcohol, other drugs, harmful relationships. Some of us became dependent on excess food.

The turning point in the lives of compulsive overeaters comes with the realization that we have a fatal disease and that without help we will be controlled by its progression. The "need" for more and more food to dull emotional pain and escape problems has put us in the position of addicts. Once we recognize the seriousness of the illness, we are ready to give wholehearted attention to arresting it.

When we are convinced emotionally as well as intellectually that our lives depend on recovering from compulsive overeating, we become willing to go to any lengths to get well. The OA program throws out a lifeline. Grabbing it and hanging on means going to meetings, getting a sponsor, calling in a food plan, learning to maintain abstinence, working the Steps, and staying in contact with the group. Sometimes schedules need to be rearranged and other activities changed. Sometimes relationships are reevaluated. We learn how to avoid situations that get us into trouble. We become willing to do whatever needs to be done in order to stay abstinent and work the program. Where life before may have been very complicated, the new one is often much more simple! Giving priority to the requirements of recovery helps to sort out everything else.

No longer will our lives be controlled by the desire for more and more food. We are going to learn how to function productively and happily without hiding in the refrigerator. The Twelve Steps guide us in getting rid of harmful dependencies and developing according to an inner pattern of positive growth. Too good to be true? We may think so until we have been in the program long enough to see with our own eyes the evidence of changed lives. We will hear stories of how despair and anxiety gradually turned to faith and confidence. We will see people living in new bodies with new mental and emotional outlooks to match.

One step at a time; one day at a time. We become new people not by willpower or by altering our environment but by first admitting that our ways have not worked and that we need help. Empty hands are necessary in order to receive the gifts of the program.

Step Two

YOU ARE NOT ALONE

Came to believe that a Power greater than ourselves could restore us to sanity.

Some of us come into the program of Overeaters Anonymous without any belief in a Power greater than ourselves. Some of us come with very strong religious convictions. Some of us are not sure. We start wherever we are—atheist, theist, agnostic, or points between. All that is required for OA membership is a desire to stop overeating. Recommended is an open mind and an attitude of willingness.

Nobody *has* to do anything in OA. The Steps are merely suggested. They outline a process that has worked for millions of addicted people, whether the problem is drugs, alcohol, food, gambling, or some other destructive crutch.

If you have trouble with the idea of God as a Higher Power, relax. Don't push it. A Higher Power for you might be the strength of the group, the strength that comes from other people who have found a solution. In taking Step One you admitted that you could not manage what you ate by yourself. Step Two is a growing belief that some force greater than your efforts will provide the strength you need. At the beginning, all that is suggested is an open mind and the willingness to believe in something more powerful than your own efforts. If you have declared bankruptcy and given up on the unsuccessful methods you have been using to try to control compulsive overeating, then Step Two is really the only solution, the only alternative to complete despair.

For most of us, seeing is believing. So our willingness to believe grows as we attend meetings and meet people who are recovering. Nothing is more convincing than to hear someone describe what they were like when they were overeating and what happened to them as a result of abstinence and the Twelve Steps. We identify with people who have the same problems we do. Their stories strike an inner chord, and we begin to think that if they found help from a Higher Power, we may too.

What Have You Got to Lose?

One thing we stand to lose by taking Step Two is the illusion of ourselves as the center of the universe. This may not be a bad idea to get rid of! When push comes to shove, do you really acknowledge any kind of force that is higher than and beyond your own ego? More than acknowledging the possibility, do you defer to such a Power in the routine situations of your everyday life? Or do you feel that a Higher Power, if indeed one exists, could not possibly be bothered by your petty concerns?

In part we may be reluctant to believe because we do not care to recognize anything greater than our own subjectivity. The ego would like to have supreme control, whatever the situation. Who wants to play a subservient role? The world encourages us to think in terms of "me first," and our psychological conditioning may make it very hard for us to get beyond our own intelligence and desires. But if there is a Power greater than ourselves, we are neither the masters of our fates nor the captains of our souls. Ouch, that hurts.

On the other hand, by ridding us of egotistical illusions, that painful piece of news enables us to live better. For one thing, we no longer have to maintain a pretense of self-sufficiency. We can ask for help. We can begin to have faith in a spiritual Power that will make us well.

Another thing we are likely to lose by taking Step Two (and continuing on with the others) is excess weight. Most of us come to the program in order to get thin, look terrific, and live happily ever after. When we lose the weight, however, most of us discover that we still have the same *living* problems we did when we were fat. It is our experience at OA that in order to cope with those problems without going back to food, we have to work the Steps. We come to OA in order to get thin, yet we stay for deeper reasons. But we do lose weight and keep it off, and that is very nice.

A great deal of fear is something that also seems to get lost as we progress through the Steps. By coming to believe in a Higher Power that *does* care about everything that happens to us, we can give up more and more of our old anxieties. Some of us have a sensation of having "come home" with the very first meeting we attend. Somehow we know that at last we are where we belong. There is an answer; there is a solution. Kindred spirits are experiencing it, and so can we. What we cannot do alone will be done for us by the strength found in the group.

Fear, self-centered pride, loneliness and isolation, resentments, anger, insecurity, hopelessness—we stand to lose varying amounts of all of these negative characteristics along with varying amounts of excess pounds. When we begin to believe that a Higher Power can restore us to sanity, anything can happen.

Who's Insane?

"Not me. I eat too much, but I'm certainly not insane. Crazy about food, maybe, but not crazy." Some of us need quite a bit of time in the program before we see just how far from sanity we were when we walked into the first meeting. We may realize our previous insanity gradually, or it may come to us in a series of sudden flashes of insight.

To begin with, most of us will readily admit to using poor judgment with regard to food and eating. We may already be convinced that the way we eat is quite irrational, if not completely crazy. Closet eating, binge eating, spending more than we can afford for food, endangering health by overeating—these are all indications that our behavior, when it comes to food, is not very sane. Since being sane means being healthy, practicing unhealthy eating habits is certainly not a sane thing to do.

Realizing the insanity in other areas of our lives may take a bit more time, but we eventually begin to see how interrelated it all is. The constant preoccupation with food and eating, the guilt and remorse after a binge, the fear of suffering because of one's inadequacies—these are all part of the insanity. So are withdrawal from those around us and feelings of depression. We get so used to the cycle of overeating, feeling bad, eating more to feel better, and feeling worse that we come to accept it as normal. It is only after a period of abstinence, when we are on the way to recovery, that we begin to see just how sick we really were.

We become aware of how we adjusted our lives to support and facilitate our overeating habits. We gradually see how this affected our relationships with family and friends, job performance, school work, what we did with spare time (if there was any left over after eating), and our emotional state. And yes, our spiritual state, too.

Another element in the insanity of compulsive overeating is fantasy. What do you think about when you are bingeing? Chances are your thoughts are not very firmly anchored in the real world. Anger and resentment can trigger fantasies of vengeance, of winning, of being "top dog." When we eat to escape reality, we often accompany the eating with fantasies of wish fulfillment. For a little while we pretend that everything is lovely. Dreams come true—until the pain of overeating brings us back to face the here and now: we have to go out to the store for more food, since we "ate the whole thing" and there is nothing left for anyone else.

When we are bingeing, especially on refined sugars and carbohydrates, our mental processes become dulled, if not completely out of whack. We are not in our right minds. We say things we don't mean, and we do things we would not do if our perceptions were not so distorted with excess calories. The mental compulsion to continue to eat food that we do not physically need is itself a form of insanity.

Being Restored

To be *restored* to sanity implies that sanity is our natural state. What is abnormal is the insanity that goes along with compulsive overeating. How do we come to believe that we were meant to be sane and not obsessed with food? This is where a Higher Power comes into the picture. Again, we need an open mind. As faith grows, we become convinced of a basic principle of goodness and health that is more powerful than any disease or distortion of the way we were meant to be. Working the program opens us to that source of health and wholeness. For most of us, the Power greater than ourselves is a loving God, as we understand the idea of God.

We do not have to subscribe to any religious creed or dogma. Our individual interpretations of God can cover a wide range of diversity. For example, someone who previously had not believed in God decided that she would imagine all the characteristics she would want God to have and think of God in those terms. She thought of God as being able to give her good things, help when she needed it, and health. Furthermore, she thought of God as *wanting* to give her these gifts, loving her, approving of her, and wanting her to be well.

A belief in the fundamental goodness of the universe is something you may not have when you come to OA. Goodness for other people, maybe, but goodness for you, doubtful. You may have such a low opinion of yourself and so much guilt that you feel you do not deserve goodness from a Higher Power. As a compulsive overeater, you may have been locked inside your disease for so long that you have lost hope of being rescued or finding a way out.

Many of us have felt this way but can affirm that we did find a way out. One phrase we heard in the meeting rooms was "Keep coming back." We did. We kept going back to meetings, sometimes one every day if we were lucky enough to live in an area where daily meetings were available. Some of us went to open Alcoholics Anonymous meetings to reinforce what we were learning about the Steps and to learn more. (In the process, some of us came to realize that we were alcoholics, too, as well as compulsive overeaters.) We got sponsors if we didn't already have them, and we began to work the program.

Being restored involves action. We act our way into right thinking, not the other way around. It is our experience that belief comes as we act, following the directions of the program. At the beginning we need only be open to the idea that there is something bigger than self. Our belief grows as we act and as our lives are changed.

"Came to Believe"

Some of us "came to" before we came to believe. We "came to" the fact that we were killing ourselves with food and hurting the people we loved with our negative emotions. "Coming to" can happen in a quick flash of insight. Coming to believe may take longer.

In many cases, even those of us who considered ourselves committed to a religious faith have decided that we were agnostic in applying that faith, since we continued to overeat compulsively. We thought we believed in God, but we didn't apply the belief to the problem that was destroying us.

None of the Twelve Steps are taken once and for all. They were set down by the first members of AA, who tried to describe the process through which they had achieved sobriety and spiritual awakening. The Steps are a guide. Not everyone follows them in the same order. Most of us go back to each one again and again as the need arises and as we are prompted by outer circumstances and an inner voice. Step Two, along with the other Steps, is something we can experience many times, frequently with an increasing depth of perception.

Action reinforces belief, and belief in turn supports action. As you look back over your life from the vantage point of abstinence and sanity, you may see that you now are learning what some part of you always knew about God but was afraid to admit. It is self-centered fear that makes us slow to believe. Once we get into the program and have friends we can talk to, some of this fear begins to dissipate. As we take action, faith grows.

Compulsive overeaters usually want everything to happen right away, if not yesterday. If belief is faltering now, we may impatiently decide that it is an impossibility. "Easy does it" is one of the many useful slogans of the program. One day at a time, one meal at a time, one Step at a time. Coming to believe may not happen overnight, but that does not mean it won't happen.

We come to believe as we hear other people talk about how they have come to believe. This program is something we "catch" through exposure to those who are living it. The fear that hampers our belief is based on pride, selfishness, and isolation. Sharing our fears and revealing our vulnerability to understanding, supportive people goes a long way toward replacing the fears with faith. "This is how it worked for me. You can do it, too. I know you can. I'll help you."

We see the program working. We hear friends tell how a Higher Power has given them abstinence and is removing their desire to overeat. They declare that they could never do this by themselves. They give examples of how this Higher Power is working out other problems in their lives. They tell us what they were like before, what happened, and what they are like now. We come to believe that a Higher Power can restore us, too, to sanity.

But often we come to believe gradually. Two years from now, when you look back at today, you will probably be amazed at how far you have come.

"I Prayed and Nothing Happened"

"I believed in God once. Sometimes I still do. But I have prayed and prayed that I would be able to eat less and lose weight, and it hasn't worked. So it's hard for me to believe, much as I'd like to."

At one time or another, most compulsive overeaters have prayed for control. When control does not come, it's easy to give up on God. Fortunately, God does not give up on us. If you have read this far, you undoubtedly have at least a small hope that the OA program will be the solution you have been searching for. That hope requires a plan of concrete action and the support of other people in order to bear fruit.

It is our experience that prayer by itself is not enough. There are things we need to do. Writing down a food plan and calling it in to a sponsor commits us more firmly to carrying out our good intentions just for today. It may be hard for you to pick up the phone and ask someone else for help. It is hard for most of us. We might like to think we can solve our problems and manage our lives without help from other people, but we admitted in Step One that we cannot.

If we do not follow the food plan today, we may be ashamed to call tomorrow and report failure. This program requires the humility to acknowledge that we are not perfect and the faith to believe that we are learning. There are no failures, only slow successes. We may have to try many, many times before we are ready for abstinence. If your sponsor is not patient, get another sponsor. God is patient.

Use the tools of recovery that the program offers. A quiet time at the beginning of the day, part of which is spent reading the literature that is available for OA and AA, becomes a daily routine that starts us off in the right frame of mind.

Going to meetings regularly and making phone calls during the day keep us on the track. Before you take that first compulsive bite, use the telephone. Write before you eat. Our Higher Power gives us abstinence and restores us to sanity, but we have to do the footwork. We are not supposed to sit back and wait for the miracle to happen. We can't do it without help from a Higher Power, but getting the help and having our prayers answered requires our cooperation.

You Are Not Alone

Before, when you were trying to escape from the insanity of compulsive overeating, you were probably trying to do it alone. When that didn't work, you may have joined a diet club for a period of time. Diet clubs may be very helpful for some people, but for a true compulsive overeater, more is necessary for recovery than diet alone. Most of us are well aware of what and how much we should eat. The problem is putting our knowledge into practice. Until we go beyond dieting and begin removing the roadblocks to emotional and spiritual growth, we will not find the strength to resist the compulsion to overeat.

As established in Step One, it is not in our power to remove the compulsion. We agree that probably no human power could do it. We came to believe "that God could and would if He were sought" (Big Book, p. 60).

Looking back from the vantage point of the program, you may come to believe that a Higher Power was taking care of you all along. This Power, greater than yourself and your compulsion, kept you from killing yourself either with food or out of despair and led you to a group of people who have found an answer. You don't have to struggle by yourself any longer. You have friends who understand you and who need your support and help as much as you need theirs.

You are not weird or beyond hope. Your problems are not unique. When you were growing up, there may not have been anyone whom you could talk to about your fears, hopes, embarrassments, and feelings of inadequacy. So you kept all of these feelings hidden, and you turned to food to ease the pain. Food may have provided temporary comfort, but it did not solve any of the problems. By keeping them to yourself and trying to ignore them by burying them in a mound of food, you cheated yourself out of valuable emotional growth. Whenever we avoid facing an uncomfortable feeling or situation, it looms even larger and more food is required to cover it up.

Turning to excess food (or to alcohol or other drugs) in order to escape the problems of living means that we inhibit emotional and spiritual development. To start growing again, we have to begin to face the problems and painful feelings rather than continue to avoid them. Some people estimate that they had an emotional age of about twelve or thirteen when they came into the program, because that was their chronological age when they stopped dealing with life and habitually numbed their feelings with food.

When the anesthetic is removed—that is, when you limit your food intake to the amounts and kinds necessary to maintain health, the buried pain is likely to surface. You are embarking on an exciting adventure—the discovery of who you really are and how you really feel! Even though it is exciting, it may hurt for a while. If the feelings had not been painful, there would have been no need to suppress them by overeating.

You are not alone in this adventure. There are other people who have been over a similar path and who can point out pitfalls and give encouragement. An OA group is especially supportive, because we identify with one another. It is a nonthreatening atmosphere, one of caring and sharing. No one has to do anything he or she is not ready to do; you progress at your own pace.

When you feel an uncontrollable craving and are ready to throw abstinence and your food plan into the nearest wastebasket, you can call someone on the phone *before* you opt for self-destruction. Talking it out with a friend who understands can shed light on what you are really feeling. Maybe you are hungry, but maybe the hunger is for something other than food. Maybe you are not hungry at all, but you are using hunger to mask deep feelings of anger that you are afraid to recognize. If you eat a dozen doughnuts, you will end up feeling angry, but it will be anger turned against yourself for eating the doughnuts, and you may never know the real reason for the anger.

Often we have been deluding ourselves for so long that without help we cannot sort out our true feelings. There is help. We do not have to keep on trying to "go it alone." The Higher Power that restores us to sanity frequently works through other people.

Sanity

Webster's dictionary defines compulsion as "an irresistible impulse to perform an irrational act." Compulsive overeaters put more and more food into their mouths, not because of physical need but because of the inability to stop eating. Being restored to sanity includes being able to eat a measured amount of food every day and then to stop eating and do something else.

In OA, part of becoming sane again involves specific actions with regard to food. Since we are powerless over it, we need some outside form of control. It is a Higher Power that removes the obsession and gives us abstinence. What we do is decide on a daily food plan and work with a qualified sponsor.

Irrational, "spontaneous," or impulse eating has been the cause of a great deal of misery for most of us. One of the ways we eliminate irrational eating is to know exactly what we are going to have for each meal each day. The plan will vary according to individual requirements and the advice of one's doctor. By writing down a plan and calling it in to a sponsor, we can let go of the obsession with what we are going to eat, one day at a time.

It is insanity for an alcoholic to take the first drink when experience indicates that the first drink will inevitably lead to getting drunk. In the same way, it is insanity for a compulsive overeater to take the first compulsive bite when experience has proved over and over again that this bite inevitably leads to a binge. Being restored to sanity means that we stop kidding ourselves that this time it will be different. When we are sane, we know that we have an illness that cannot be cured but can be controlled by abstinence and the Twelve Steps. We know that the first compulsive bite will eventually become a binge. No matter how thin we are or how long we have been in the program, we remain compulsive overeaters. For us, snacks and between-meal nibbling are insane, since they trigger the obsession, and sooner or later (usually sooner) we are right back into uncontrolled eating.

Working the Steps of this program results in a new attitude of humility, which is also part of sanity for a compulsive overeater. The ego trips of the past invariably got us into trouble. Ego trips and binges often went hand in hand and removed us further and further from reality.

Our past insanity probably included wide swings of mood. We were either the greatest or the worst, fantastic or hopeless. Sanity puts us in a comfortable place where we can accept ourselves as people with strengths and weaknesses, not perfect but learning.

Sanity means living in the real world instead of in a fantasy. Daydreaming of all of the marvelous things that will happen to you when you are thin, and eating while you daydream, is living in a crazy world. So is the habit of mentally rearranging circumstances to suit yourself. In this program we pray for the sanity to accept the things we cannot change; we stop trying to wish them away or eat them away. The courage to change what we can and the wisdom to know the difference are also part of the sanity given back to us by a Higher Power who does not intend us to be obsessed with eating.

"Greater than Ourselves"

Surrender and humility are crucial to all of the Steps. As long as we are caught up in self-centered pride, we cannot ask for help. As long as we think of ourselves as the center of the universe, there is no room for a Higher Power. If we insist on muddling through, "controlling" what we eat "our way," the illness gets worse. Compulsive overeating is a progressive disease that is physical, emotional, and spiritual. Like recovering alcoholics, those whose disease has been successfully arrested describe what has happened to them in terms of a "spiritual awakening." By means of spiritual growth, the compulsion to overeat was removed.

You may feel at this point that a spiritual awakening is low on your list of priorities, that all you want to do is stop overeating and lose weight, never mind the spirituality. That's what most of us wanted. Most of us found, however, that nothing worked until we stopped relying on material solutions and became willing to grow spiritually. The alternatives are fairly clear-cut: spiritual growth or physical destruction. Which do you choose?

How the spiritual awakening is experienced varies from person to person. Stories in the Big Book of Alcoholics Anonymous and in the book *Overeaters Anonymous** run the gamut from dramatic moments of illumination to slow processes of gradually developing faith. What is agreed on is that a Power greater than the individual has effected a change. And that's what we are after in the first place, isn't it? A change in behavior so that we are no longer controlled by the compulsion to overeat.

We may not understand how the spiritual Power works. One doesn't have to understand how electricity works in order to use it. The Higher Power of our understanding may be anything from a vague idea of a spirit that infuses the group to a Supreme Being as described in a particular religious creed. Whatever it is, it is greater than our individual selves and does for us what we cannot do alone: It removes the compulsion to overeat and restores us to useful, fulfilling, and happy lives.

---

* Torrance, CA: O.A. World Service Office, 1980.

Step Three

GIVING UP THE GAME

Made a decision to turn our will and our lives over to the care of God *as we understood Him.*

Step Three begins a process of active commitment to the Overeaters Anonymous program. Whereas we were in a passive position for Steps One and Two—admitting powerlessness and acknowledging a Higher Power—in Step Three we make a positive, active decision that will affect every area of life. It is a decision we renew on a daily basis.

For some of us, making the decision seems like jumping off the edge of a cliff. We would probably never be willing to take this "leap of faith" if the pain of hanging on to our old ways had not become greater than the fear of letting go.

"Trust God to take care of my life? How do I know he will? I'm not even sure there is a God." Trusting a Higher Power may be very hard for you to do. But if you are truly desperate, you may be willing to try it anyway, on the recommendation of people who can vouch for the fact that it has worked for them. You can start with just a tiny bit of willingness to trust. As you take the risk and as you see that it makes a positive difference in your life, your level of trust rises.

Remember, this is a one-day-at-a-time program. What may seem clearly "impossible for the rest of my life" *can* be done just for today. *Today* I can take Step Three. I can decide to turn my will and my life over to the care of the God of my understanding just for today. I don't have to worry about tomorrow. I may get run over by a bus tomorrow. Or I may never make it through tonight. All I have is now, today. If I can trust providence to take care of me now, chances are that I will also be able to trust tomorrow, and the next day, one day at a time.

As compulsive people, we grasp for certainty. We would like to have everything nailed down—to know where we will be ten years from now and to be certain that everything will be fine. Part of our irrational overeating is undoubtedly an attempt to find certainty and assurance in food. But the only solid result of overeating is fat!

Deciding to trust God instead of food is a one-hundred-eighty-degree turnaround in attitude. We are changing from a material orientation to a spiritual one. And we may fear that if the bottom falls out of this rather shaky Higher Power business, we will be left exposed and defenseless.

What is the alternative? We can continue to try to manage our own lives and continue searching for a way to stop overeating. We can continue to trust food, money, intelligence, willpower, sex, good business connections, family, friends, a psychiatrist, and so forth to solve our problems and make us happy. Not that all of these things aren't important and helpful—they are. But are they filling the emptiness? Has trying to run our own lives produced inner peace? Can we stop overeating without a Power greater than ourselves?

If, after an honest evaluation, we conclude that we have made rather a mess of things by ourselves, Step Three begins to look like a practical move. Turning our wills and our lives over to God means finally establishing them on a firm foundation. The shaky foundation was our own willfulness. Surrendering self-will and letting a Higher Power run our lives is the core of the program that promises us freedom from compulsive overeating.

Turning It Over

"It's out of control, H. P. The food, my relationships, my work—everything. You'll have to take over. I'm tired. I can't do anything right. I'm scared. I'm confused. I should have stayed in bed this morning. I'll never get through the day. Help!"

So it goes. Each day that we ask for help, we strengthen our conscious commitment to spiritual growth. Each time we try it, the answers become more clear. One day at a time, we allow our self-will to conform more closely to God's will.

Not ready for that kind of commitment? Are you ready to make a beginning? Are you willing to go along with the idea that whatever plan a Higher Power has for your life, it probably does not include compulsive overeating? If so, doesn't it seem reasonable that God will make available to you the strength to resist the first compulsive bite, as long as you are sincerely trying to follow God's plan for your life?

We grow up with the idea that *we* should make the plans, decide where we are going, satisfy our desires, actualize ourselves. "What do *I* want to do with *my* life?" But as long as the accent is on I, me, mine, we are limiting our potential for growth. We discover that we want one thing today and another tomorrow. Self-actualizing with only our own limited power may not get us very far.

In fact, most of us find that living according to the capricious dictates of self-will leads to messed-up relationships with other people and enslavement to out-of-control appetites. We get bogged down in destructive dependencies—in the case of the compulsive overeater, excess food. Fear and anxiety increase.

Then what happens? Either we continue down the path of addiction—a circular path, since we feel bad when we overeat and then we eat more to feel better—or we get outside help.

When we decide that using excess food to reduce fear and anxiety does not work and is slowly destroying us, we have to find another way of coping with these feelings. The Twelve Step program shows us how to live without using excess food as a crutch. We turn the eating problem over to a Higher Power, since we cannot solve it ourselves. We turn over all of the other aspects of our lives, too, since we have come to believe that God can do a better job of managing and directing them than we can.

One Day at a Time

Living the third Step means learning how to live one day at a time. When we are in tune with a Higher Power, we are living in the present instead of fretting over the past or fantasizing about the future. God is now. God gives us strength for what actually is happening right this minute. When we try to rewrite what happened a long time ago or when we worry about what might happen tomorrow, we lose touch with our source of strength. Wandering around in a daydream makes it easy to get lost.

We can't know what tomorrow will bring. The best way to prepare for whatever may arrive is to maintain spiritual contact today. Amazingly, when we stay attuned to a Higher Power today, whatever comes up tomorrow turns out to be okay. Often it's even better than okay—a lot better.

It stands to reason that a Higher Power has access to information that you and I do not have. If we insist on acting only according to our limited vision, we restrict ourselves. Turning our lives over to the care of the God of our understanding frees us from our own limitations. If we are listening now, one day at a time, to inner promptings, we become more creative. The pieces begin to fall into place. Situations that seemed impossible begin to untangle. We get the strength and the insight to deal with them on a daily basis.

One day at a time, one meal at a time. For the compulsive overeater, nothing is more important than staying in the here and now. I cannot conceive of being abstinent for the rest of my life, but with God's help and the support of the group I can be abstinent just for today. I can abstain from this meal to the next. I have a food plan for today, and I will not worry about being hungry tomorrow or bingeing tomorrow. If I feel hungry this afternoon, I know that I will survive until dinner. After dinner, it is not likely that I will die of starvation before morning.

I believe that it is not God's will for me to overeat, and so I do today what is necessary to ensure that I will not take the first compulsive bite. I know what I will eat for breakfast, lunch, and dinner. I make phone calls to friends in the program, go to meetings, read the literature, spend time keeping in touch with my Higher Power. I remember the *how* of the program: honesty, openmindedness, willingness. By doing this today, one day at a time, I can trust that the God who takes care of me today will also take care of me tomorrow.

Rebellion

I trust, but at the same time I rebel — rebel against writing down a food plan, against calling it in to a sponsor, against following it, against letting God manage my life. Whatever it is, I want to do it my way. I want what I want when I want it — *now*, if not yesterday.

Overeating is a classic form of rebellion. Ever since Eve ate the apple, forbidden fruit has symbolized temptation. As soon as you try to go on a diet, everything that is not on it becomes much more desirable than before. That is one reason why diets do not work for compulsive overeaters. For us, a diet is definitely not enough.

Writing down a food plan can also generate rebellion. It is as though inside many of us there is a streak of obstinate perversity that drives us to do the opposite of what we know we should be doing. We refuse to be told how to behave. Even when we tell *ourselves* "Three meals a day," we can react like children rebelling against their parents.

We become split personalities, at war with ourselves. One voice says, "No, don't take the first compulsive bite!" while another voice screams, "Don't restrain yourself—indulge at any cost!" "You've had your measured meal and that's enough." "Just a little taste won't hurt." "Stop eating!" "Do what you jolly well please—nobody can stop you!"

The compulsion is baffling and cunning. It deludes us into thinking that this time we can get away with a little extra. "What am I, a robot or something? I don't need to weigh and measure all the time. I can exercise some judgment and be a little flexible today. I'll make up for it tomorrow." Then the little extra bite takes over and becomes a binge.

Self-will rebels at the idea of being directed by a Higher Power. It rebels against the existence of anything greater than itself. Self-will and appetite are closely connected. They line themselves up against the voices of reason and experience.

We can continue to rebel and continue down the path of self-destruction. We can continue to live lives of quiet desperation. We can follow our compulsion into insanity and death. As free agents, we can choose. Nobody, least of all God, is forcing us to surrender our will and our lives.

What is inevitable is that the illness of compulsive overeating will get worse if not arrested. The course the illness takes is variable, depending on individual factors. Sometimes it leads to slow death from obesity-related diseases; sometimes it leads to sudden death due to cardiac arrest or esophageal rupture.

Fortunately, many of us realize where we are headed at an early stage of the illness. When we see where self-will is leading us, by the grace of God the wind goes out of our rebellious sails, and we run up the white flag of surrender.

Moment of Decision

Once convinced that our self-will will eventually destroy us, we make the "decision to turn our will and our lives over to the care of God as we understood Him." In the words of the Big Book of Alcoholics Anonymous, "We had to quit playing God. It didn't work" (Big Book, p. 62).

When we make this decision—when we take Step Three—we sign on with "a new Employer." From now on, we know that a Higher Power is running the show, and we can relax. Playing God is hard work; maintaining the illusion of control involves tremendous fear and anxiety. It is a great relief to be able to give up the game.

You may want to take Step Three with your sponsor or someone else who is close to you. The following prayer is suggested in the Big Book. (Remember, this is to the God of *your understanding*.)

> God, I offer myself to Thee—to build with me and to do with me as Thou wilt. Relieve me of the bondage of self, that I may better do Thy will. Take away my difficulties, that victory over them may bear witness to those I would help, of Thy Power, Thy Love, and Thy Way of Life. May I do Thy Will always! (Big Book, p. 63)

If you don't like that prayer, don't say it. Everything in the program is merely suggested as an example of what has worked for others. You do not need to say any formal prayer. Making the Step Three decision can happen on a very deep, intuitive level without words. In a flash, you can decide to change from being ego-directed to being spiritually prompted. You may find, however, that consciously verbalizing the decision nails down the change in attitude. Then, when you are emotionally upset and things are getting out of hand, you can remind yourself of the concrete decision you have made to let a Higher Power run the show.

Step Three simplifies life considerably. It means that whatever the circumstances, our main intent is to know God's will for us and do it. Everything else will take care of itself.

Freedom

It is a paradox that the harder we try to find freedom and pleasure by indulging our wants, the more enslaved and unhappy we become. The longer we work this program, the more firmly convinced we are that trying to go against God's will is at the root of our dissatisfaction and frustration. To be hooked on oneself is perhaps the worst addiction of all! Working through substance addiction—whether it be alcohol abuse, drug abuse, or food abuse—brings all of us into a confrontation with self-centeredness.

Freedom from "the bondage of self" is what we are asking for in Step Three and what the program promises us. Self-centeredness has driven us to the wall. We have tried to make ourselves happy by every conceivable means and find that the harder we try, the more miserable we become. One minute we think we will be happy if we can just be thin; the next minute, all we want is a pizza. A little while later, more money appears to be the solution to every problem. Then more love, more sex, more power. The list goes on and on.

In order to make ourselves happy, we try to control not only our own lives but everyone else's too—especially the lives of those we love. We think we know best. We have the mistaken idea that power and control will give us freedom, when in fact the effort to hang on makes us fearful and anxious. Trying to manipulate others wastes energy and invites frustration.

The only way to be free is to go along with the Power that governs the universe. Fighting God's will for us is a losing battle. When my will is in harmony with the will of this Higher Power, I am free to be who I really am and do what I am supposed to do. I do not have to work out elaborate strategies to try to make things go my way. I do not have to worry about imminent disaster. Whatever happens will be right when I am sincerely trying to know and do God's will.

Freedom from self-will run riot includes freedom from compulsive overeating. The compulsion may not be lifted immediately upon our taking the third Step, but we are laying the groundwork that is crucial to maintaining abstinence. It is possible, though, for the compulsion to be lifted *before* we take the third Step. This thing we call abstinence is a gift given to us daily, and it depends on our spiritual condition. Turning our lives over to a spiritual Power one day at a time will eventually give us the strength to stop eating compulsively.

What we sought in excess food was not to be found there. We were not satisfied; we wanted something more. Getting into the program and beginning to work the Steps gives us glimpses of a spiritual life that is qualitatively different from the life we were living before. This is not something more, not something added on to everything else we have. It is something entirely new, and it satisfies our hunger in a way that more food never did.

Abstinence alone is not enough. We need to live *for* something. Through the program, we learn to live for, and by, a Power greater than ourselves. This brings us the satisfaction, peace, and love that we lacked, so we no longer need to overeat.

Sound impossible? Wishful thinking? Try it. If you do not like the new life, your former misery will be refunded.

Freedom from the bondage of self eventually brings freedom from craving and freedom from fear. That is what results when we allow a Higher Power to direct us.

Of course, all of this does not happen immediately. Spiritual growth may be slow, but it is solid. As we look back on our lives, we see that God gives us what we need when we are ready for it. God's timetable may surprise us, and we may not think we want all of what comes our way. We may get impatient and try to take back control. Then we are no longer free. We get entangled in the same old snarl of self-will.

But once having tasted the freedom that comes with surrender, we are never the same. We do not want to go back to the old life of rebellious indulgence. We've glimpsed the light at the end of the tunnel, and we are being pulled forward, drawn toward that light in spite of doubts and reservations that may still linger. The doubts will gradually fade as we experience the trust and freedom that we gain from surrendering to a Higher Power.

A Commitment to Abstinence

"Deep down in every man, woman, and child is the fundamental idea of God" (Big Book, p. 55). We can find the "Great Reality deep down within us." When we find it, our entire attitude toward life is changed, and the miracle of healing can occur.

Making the decision to trust God with our lives—the small events as well as the big ones—opens the way to a fuller understanding of this Great Reality within us. When we make a third Step commitment, we open the channels to God's power. We become convinced on a gut level that compulsive overeating is contrary to God's will for our lives and, indeed, prevents us from living according to God's direction. Therefore, turning our wills and our lives over to God's care involves a commitment to abstinence as the will of our Higher Power.

Abstinence is something we practice regardless of how we feel. No matter how down or how great we feel, or even if we don't feel anything at all, we can maintain abstinence. The strength to do it comes from a

Higher Power, and abstinence is ours to enjoy as long as we stay attuned to that source of strength. We do not even have to enjoy it, but if we think back to our bingeing and the misery we experienced then, *enjoyment* will, by comparison, seem a mild way to describe the new state.

We all know what happens if we lose abstinence. Food then takes the place of God, and the craving for more controls our lives. Energy and enthusiasm dissolve, each day becomes a chore, and chaos returns. If we let go of abstinence, we can never be sure whether we will get it back again. What first compulsive bite is worth the wreckage?

Being committed to abstinence means giving it priority. For a compulsive overeater, no other consideration is more important. In times of trouble and in times of joy, our survival depends on our remembering that we are compulsive overeaters and that abstinence comes first. To take the illness lightly or to think that we can get away with some cheating here and there is to forget that it is a progressive disease. Even after a long period of abstinence, if we return to compulsive overeating, we find that our binges are worse and the insanity is greater.

Committing ourselves to abstinence also means that we accept whatever discomfort or inconvenience may go along with it. We may have periods of hunger, depression, boredom, anxiety. We will undoubtedly have to face painful feelings that we formerly buried under a mountain of excess food. We may have to make special arrangements to ensure that the food on our plan will be available when we need it. We become willing to go to any lengths in order to recover.

Food can no longer be an option when we are feeling bad or at loose ends. What do you turn to instead? OA gives us a support group. There are people to call and there is literature to read. We learn, moreover, that nothing ensures our own abstinence better than working with and being of service to other compulsive overeaters.

We can turn to the group and we can turn to a Higher Power, letting go of our problems and praying for strength to carry out God's will for our lives. We can be willing to hurt for a while as a small price to pay for recovery.

It is habit that lures us back into the old ways and tempts us to self-destruct. Once upon a time, compulsive overeating was fun, and we would like to recapture that pleasure. We need to remember that the fun part is over and that from now on the first compulsive bite will always bring pain.

When the pain of overeating is worse than the pain of abstaining, we are on the way to recovery. Abstinence may not be much fun, but it is infinitely preferable to ever-worsening binges. Since most of us find that we cannot abstain without the help of a Higher Power, the commitment to abstinence ensures that we are going to grow in our relationship to the God of our understanding. We have to ask for the strength to be abstinent on a daily basis, sometimes much more often. This keeps us in contact with a spiritual Power and keeps us growing.

Taking It Back

Okay, so you took Step Three, you became abstinent, and everything was fine for a few days, weeks, months, perhaps even years. Then something happened. Maybe you forgot that you were a compulsive overeater. Maybe you let some other part of your life become more important than maintaining abstinence. Maybe you forgot about your Higher Power.

At any rate, you lost your abstinence and you took back not only the eating problem but also the living problem. It could be that it happened the other way around – that you tried to take back control of other areas of your life such as sex, money, or work, and before long you discovered that your abstinence was slipping.

Basically it all boils down to whether we are letting God have control or whether we are trying to manage everything ourselves. We have proved over and over again that the first way works and the second does not.

So why do we take back all the problems? Before coming down on ourselves too hard, it's good to remember that we expect progress, not perfection. The program is a way of life that is very different from the way most of us were living previously, and it often takes time to make such a radical change. As long as we live, we will probably have to deal with the tendency to be self-centered rather than God-centered. It keeps cropping up and getting us into trouble.

The difference is that we now know what to do when we start to fall apart. We can get back to meetings, call our sponsors and other program friends, and spend more time getting in touch with a Higher Power. A slip does not need to plunge us into despair. Abstinence is something we are given every minute of every day. We can reach out and receive it at 11:00 A.M. or 4:00 P.M. or 9:30 P.M., even if we have temporarily taken back the problem of compulsive overeating. We now know where the answer is, and with practice we will develop our ability to live this new life.

Most of us find that as we spend more time in the program, the intensity of our problems lessens. There is always room for growth, and as we clear one hurdle, another one usually arises. This may also happen with regard to food—we get the refined sugars out of our lives, but we are tempted to binge on cottage cheese. Bingeing on cottage cheese is still compulsive overeating, but the hangover is considerably less severe than the hangover from refined sugar.

What we are aiming for is the ability to put food in its proper place, to eat three measured meals a day with no snacks, and to place every area of our life under God's direction. We would probably never be willing to attempt any of this if there were an easier way to survive. But we find that we cannot maintain abstinence from compulsive overeating (which would kill us sooner or later) unless we are also working toward being honest in our relationships with other people, restrained in our demands for material gain, less selfish in expressing sexuality and ambition. The list could go on indefinitely, but this is not just another self-improvement program. The growth comes as we are ready for it, and we do not achieve it by ourselves; our Higher Power gives us only what we can handle one day at a time.

For some reason, some of us seem to have to go backward for a while in order to move forward again with renewed vigor. "Taking it back" reminds us graphically and painfully of how miserable the old way is and how much we need to concentrate on applying Step Three in every circumstance.

Surrender

"I forget to ask"

"Take over, H. P. I'm stuck again, and I can't move forward without you. I know you're there. The problem is that I forgot to listen. I get swept up in a hurricane of what *I want*. It can destroy me—that I know."

"I want" is very strong. It becomes "I want more and more." Allowed to grow unchecked, it will drive me to insanity or death. I cannot control this "I want" force by willpower, but I can surrender and relinquish it to the God of my understanding. When it comes back, I can turn it over again, every day, many times a day. Each time I turn it over, I am building up the habit of avoiding the self-will trap. Each time I surrender, I am learning to rely on the strength that comes from my Higher Power.

Part of growing up is accepting the fact that we cannot have everything we want. "God, grant me the serenity to accept the things I cannot change, the courage to change the things I can, and the wisdom to know the difference." As our will comes into harmony with God's will for us, our lives reflect new confidence, new freedom, and new peace.

FACE TO FACE WITH YOURSELF

Made a searching and fearless moral inventory of ourselves.

Congratulations. The first three Steps in the program for compulsive overeaters have brought you to a new place. You have admitted the fact that once you take the first compulsive bite you are powerless over food. You have admitted that you need help, and you have become willing to seek that help from a Power greater than yourself. You have decided to try letting your Higher Power manage your life.

When we make the decision to turn our wills and our lives over to the care of God as we understand him (Step Three), the next question becomes, "How do we actually do that on a day-to-day basis?" The answers are found in Steps Four through Twelve. These remaining Steps of the program contain the directions for following through on the decision made in Step Three, which is very possibly the most important decision we will ever make.

Remember, the program is a matter of choice. None of us *has* to follow the directions—they are merely suggested. What they offer is a way of life that is bringing recovery to a great number of people like ourselves, people who are suffering from addictive behavior, whether the addiction is to compulsive overeating, alcohol, gambling, drugs, or something else.

So here you are, wanting recovery and ready to take the fourth Step: to make "a searching and fearless moral inventory" of yourself. Why is it necessary to make such an inventory? Since the business of your life has not been operating to your satisfaction, you are turning it over to new management. The first thing to do is to take stock of *what* you are turning over. Then, under the direction of the new Manager, you will be able to clean out the shop and to begin getting rid of whatever needs to go.

Taking a commercial inventory is a fact-finding and a fact-facing process. It is an effort to discover the truth about the stock-in-trade. One object is to disclose damaged to unsalable goods, to get rid of them promptly and without regret. If the owner of the business is to be successful, he cannot fool himself about values. (Big Book, p. 64)

When we take the fourth Step personal inventory, we sit down and make an honest appraisal and evaluation of what is going on in our lives: our assets and our liabilities, our values and our success in living up to them. How long has it been since you seriously took stock of who you are, where you are, and where you are going? Don't be overwhelmed by the immensity of the task, and don't let fear or pride persuade you to procrastinate. Getting started is the hardest part. Once you decide to begin, the inventory will unfold as you go along—one word at a time, one sentence at a time, one topic at a time. Think about Step Four as an adventure in self-discovery.

Does the inventory have to be written? Yes. It is the process of actually putting thoughts down on paper that makes the investigation a thorough and comprehensive one. Writing often uncovers insights not realized by thought alone. This may be the first time you have taken the opportunity to organize yourself on paper and examine the results. Writing an inventory is a chance to pinpoint behaviors and feelings that have been bothering you. Then you can examine those behaviors and feelings in the conscious light of day instead of allowing them to nag at you from the shadows of your awareness and sabotage your efforts to progress. In the *Twelve Steps and Twelve Traditions*, the writing experience is described as "an aid to clear thinking and honest appraisal. It will be the first tangible evidence of our complete willingness to move forward" (Twelve and Twelve, p. 55).

We demonstrate our determination to follow this program of recovery by getting out pencil and paper and beginning to write. The inventory is a searching one, not a superficial jotting down of generalities. *Searching* means that we will set aside a generous amount of time, probe deeply into our thoughts and actions, record specific examples of behavior, be objective in our analysis as far as possible, and above all, be honest. We can take stock fearlessly, because we know we have the support and love of a Higher Power. We will not avoid facing the truth about ourselves. Our Higher Power will show us what we need to see and will strengthen us to accept ourselves as we are. Since we have turned over our lives and our wills to God's care, we have nothing to fear.

Confidence and courage come from knowing that our efforts are being directed by a Power greater than ourselves.

As compulsive overeaters, we continually tried to bury our problems under a mountain of excess food. We would not face ourselves and our negative emotions—resentment, arrogance, fear, guilt, anger, hurt, shame. Instead of recognizing and dealing with these feelings and our self-destructive actions, we told ourselves and everyone else that all was well, and we ate. Food may temporarily dull the pain of living, but it is not a permanent solution for emotional distress or counterproductive behavior. Excess food only obscures the issue; it keeps us from understanding the real problems.

In order to live without resorting to extra calories whenever we are disturbed, we need to analyze what it is about our personalities and our ways of reacting to people and events that should be changed. Our old ways have not worked. Very early in life we may have fallen into the habit of eating to avoid feeling pain. This short-circuited the process of growing up emotionally.

Becoming emotionally and spiritually mature enough to deal with life without overeating is our present goal. Before we are finished with Step Four, we are going to discover where we have been sabotaging ourselves and how we can begin to exchange our liabilities for assets.

The following guide is suggested to help you with your inventory. Each of the five sections includes questions to ask yourself about specific attitudes and actions that are part of your character and your everyday life. Allowing ample time to be thoughtful and thorough, write down your answers, giving concrete examples. (Use additional paper as needed.)

1. Being Honest

We are often reminded at meetings of Overeaters Anonymous that success in this program depends on rigorous honesty. We may have tried to fool ourselves and others in the past, but we now realize that our recovery requires us to "tell it like it is."

Has dishonesty been a part of your pattern of compulsive overeating? In what way? Have you been a sneak eater? Have you stolen money to buy food—or even just stolen food? Are you honest with yourself now about what you eat?

In your relationships with other people, are there experiences from the past involving dishonesty or cheating on your part that continue to bother you today? Describe these events and feelings.

Is it a relief to be able to share honestly at meetings? With your sponsor? Give an example of a recent situation in which choosing to be open and truthful has improved a relationship.

How have you kidded yourself by hiding, making alibis, rationalizing, justifying, telling half-truths, being phony, minimizing, conning, and breaking promises? Give an example of how working the program is helping you to get rid of illusions about yourself and others.

Facing the truth about ourselves—taking responsibility for what we feel, say, and do—is a liberating experience. We do not have to cover up our mistakes and pretend to be perfect. Since our Higher Power accepts us and is on our side, we can find out who we really are and be that person. In the adventure of self-discovery, the insights come as we are ready to receive them. Some of the truth about ourselves may be painful, but God never gives us more than we are able to handle. The truth will set us free.

2. Acknowledging Anger and Resentment

"Eating over it" was a conditioned response for many of us. Often we did not even know we were angry—our bodies translated the uncomfortable and threatening feelings into hunger. We may have eaten voraciously, venting the anger on the food we were devouring and on the bodies we were damaging, without conscious awareness of what was really troubling us.

Resentment is the "number one" offender. . . . In dealing with resentments, we set them on paper. We listed people, institutions or principles with whom we were angry. In most cases it was found that our self-esteem, our pocketbooks, our ambitions, our personal relationships (including sex) were hurt or threatened. (Twelve and Twelve, pp. 64–65)

Are you angry right now with someone close to you? Why? (Remember, you are taking *your* inventory, not someone else's. Focus on your feelings and reactions rather than on the other person's character defects.) How are you dealing with the anger?

Do you hang on to anger, allowing it to fester into long-term resentment? Give a specific example, telling who, where, when, why, and how long. How does this affect you emotionally and spiritually?

How is a temper tantrum like an eating binge? Explain by relating a personal experience. Is "justified" anger worth the price? Who suffers most, you or the object of your ire?

How does it feel to let go of a resentment? What do you stand to lose? To gain?

Sometimes when we take Step Three, we hold back part of our anger and resentment for a rainy day instead of turning it all over, along with the rest of our lives. If we find ourselves propelled to the refrigerator when these negative feelings surface, we will be strongly motivated to get rid of them in order to maintain abstinence and peace of mind. Think about the rewards you get from substituting forgiveness and understanding for anger and resentment. With the help of your Higher Power, are you increasingly able to let go of your anger in exchange for serenity? Write down a possible future situation in which this could happen.

3. Recognizing False Pride

Pride . . . is a basic breeder of most human difficulties, the chief block to true progress. Pride lures us into making demands upon ourselves or upon others which cannot be met without perverting or misusing our God-given instincts. When the satisfaction of our instincts for sex, security, and a place in society becomes the primary object of our lives, then pride steps in to justify our excesses. (Twelve and Twelve, p. 50)

We discover that false pride and egotism have been responsible for much of our unhappiness and crazy behavior. How have you been sabotaged by pride and self-centeredness? Are they operating in your life right now? What about grandiosity? Give examples of how you have placed yourself above others.

In the past, did excessive pride bind you to impossibly high standards of perfection? When they were not met, did the failure become an excuse to overeat for consolation? Does pride make you afraid to try for fear of failing? Describe your experiences.

How has false pride kept you from reaching out to other people?

Are you finding it easier now to admit mistakes and acknowledge yourself as you are so that you can begin to change? To ask for help when you need it? Give examples.

The Twelve Step program is a journey that gradually releases us from false pride and egotism and leads us to a healthy dependence on a Power greater than ourselves. Taking this inventory is, in itself, an ego-puncturing experience. Isn't it a relief to stop pretending to be perfect, to quit trying to do everything by yourself? Describe an example.

4. Exchanging Fear and Self-Pity for Faith and Gratitude

In the words of the *Twelve Steps and Twelve Traditions,*

The chief activator of our defects has been self-centered fear—primarily fear that we would lose something we already possessed or would fail to get something we demanded. Living upon a basis of unsatisfied demands, we were in a state of continual disturbance and frustration. Therefore, no peace was to be had unless we could find a means of reducing these demands. (Twelve and Twelve, pp. 77–78)

When we are afraid, the natural response is to run away or to become paralyzed. Unacknowledged fears grow bigger and bigger, and the compulsive overeater requires more and more food to keep them at bay. What are some of your secret fears? Which ones are based on fact and which are irrational?

Are feelings of guilt contributing to your fears? In what way? How does the program help you to let go of guilt?

Describe how a growing belief in the care of a Higher Power diminishes your fears. What does it mean to you to "let go and let God"? Give an example of accepting a situation you cannot change. As you trust God more, are you also able to have more faith in yourself? How?

Letting our unsatisfied demands be the basis of our lives opens the door to self-pity. Instead of appreciating what we have, we think about what we don't have and feel sorry for ourselves. What a waste of time and energy! Has gratitude been a missing ingredient in your life? Can you think of an occasion in the recent past when you played the game of "poor me"? Describe it.

What does it mean to you to be a *gratefully* recovering compulsive overeater? What are some of the benefits that have already come to you through the program? Are you finding a means of reducing your unsatisfied demands?

Make a list of the good things in your life. How can you focus on them when self-pity threatens to attack?

List three specific ways you can express gratitude today. How does abstinence fit in?

5. Choosing to Share

The great "I want" cuts us off from satisfying interpersonal relationships and blinds us to the needs and gifts of other people. Describe your personal experience with self-will run riot and out-of-control instincts of self-gratification.

What are your standards for a sharing and caring expression of your sexuality? How does your behavior conform to these standards?

Were isolation and withdrawal part of your pattern of compulsive overeating? How did this affect the people around you? How did it affect you? Is the program helping you to reach out and share? How?

As you become more accepting of yourself, are you able to be more tolerant and patient with others? Less selfish and more giving? Explain.

Are you willing to share this inventory? With whom? Describe the mutual benefits that you and the other person will derive from the experience of open and honest communication on a deeply meaningful level.

Since these questions do not, by any means, exhaust the possible topics that may be included in a fourth Step inventory, you may wish to explore additional areas of your character and behavior. Your inventory, however, does not have to be perfect, nor does it have to be a literary masterpiece. What counts is that now you have done your best to look searchingly at your actions, motives, and values and to analyze them honestly.

How committed are you to emotional and spiritual growth? When you feel yourself beginning to slip into an old self-destructive attitude or action, are you willing to stop for a moment and think about the consequences and the alternatives? Are you willing to ask yourself if there is a better way? Are you willing to ask a Higher Power for help?

You can choose to change and grow. Maintaining contact with the God of your understanding, the new Manager of your life, is the key to trading liabilities for assets as you move through the Steps of the program.

AND THE TRUTH WILL SET YOU FREE

Admitted to God, to ourselves, and to another human being, the exact nature of our wrongs.

"We must be entirely honest with somebody if we expect to live long or happily in this world" (Big Book, p. 73). Many of us would add: and if we expect to recover from compulsive overeating and maintain long-term abstinence and serenity, the same rule applies.

Step Five can be a turning point for those of us who have felt alienated from a Higher Power, ourselves, and other people. Candidly telling another person everything in our fourth Step inventory fosters a deep sense of healing and belonging. Maybe we do not fully know ourselves. Nor can we entirely accept ourselves until we put our thoughts and feelings into words and share our self-discovery with someone else.

"Until we actually sit down and talk about what we have so long hidden, our willingness to clean house is still largely theoretical. When we are honest with another person, it confirms that we have been honest with ourselves and with God" (Twelve and Twelve, p. 61).

The object of Steps Four and Five is not to become martyrs or to put ourselves down in a masochistic way. Rather, the purpose is to become aware of the ways in which we sabotage our ability to change.

Fear and anxiety result from trying to cover up our defects and our liabilities. We live with an everpresent threat of exposure. But when we are completely honest with a sympathetic friend or counselor, when we carefully examine the problem areas of our behavior and balance our liabilities against our current assets or those we are trying to develop, we no longer have anything to hide. What a relief! Taking responsibility, out loud, for what we have done and left undone starts the process of changing what we don't like about ourselves.

For many of us, sharing our inventory with someone we respect and trust, and feeling understood and accepted by that person, is the beginning of what the program describes as a spiritual awakening. The experience of forgiveness and reconciliation marks a turning point in our lives.

Admitting to God and Ourselves

Before we found the program, some of us spent a good part of our lives trying to run away from our Higher Power as well as from our inner selves. Much of our difficulty with the idea of a Higher Power is caused by pride. For years we have been intent on proving how well we could get along on our own, without God as we understand him, and without listening to an inner voice. It takes humility to admit, "Okay, H. P., I've really made a mess of things. I've flunked out of school because I wasn't willing to work, and I've damaged my body by habitual self-indulgence." Or to admit, "I see that my petty resentment and jealousy have been a major cause of the strained relationship between my brother and me. I've been a real pain." Humility is part of recovery.

So the first thing that Step Five suggests we do is admit to God and to ourselves just where we have gone off the track. You may be asking, "Isn't that a little silly? I can't tell my Higher Power or myself anything we don't already know."

True. But if you have thoroughly worked the preceding Steps, you are developing a new, more meaningful relationship with the God of your understanding. And you are learning to be more honest with yourself. You have learned that others have recovered through trust in a Higher Power and an honest effort to be open to inner guidance from that Higher Power.

Admitting to God the exact nature of our wrongs puts us in an immediate relationship with our Higher Power. It is a right relationship, because we are acknowledging that we haven't done well on our own and that we need help. Admitting our mistakes usually brings up feelings of regret and remorse. That's painful. But unless we are willing to take responsibility for our actions, we will continue to run away from reality. When we accept the truth—both its pleasant and unpleasant aspects—we can experience the acceptance and forgiveness of a Higher Power. Then we can forgive and accept ourselves.

Seeing who we really are, what assets and liabilities we have, liberates us from the game of trying to fool ourselves. We may have made a considerable effort to ignore and forget behavior that has embarrassed us and made us ashamed. Perhaps we have tended to blame anyone and everyone else for our problems, blinding ourselves to our own responsibility for them. In this program, we learn that we cannot change other people. We are not responsible for what they do. We are, however, responsible for what we do and how we *react* to what others do. Through the help of a Higher Power, we can change our own behavior.

Seeking Another Human Being

"Somehow, being alone with God doesn't seem as embarrassing as facing up to another person" (Twelve and Twelve, p. 61).

Do you have the feeling that you have always been different from "normal" people? That if others knew you as you really are, they would quickly reject you? Does being around people seem to require an exhausting effort for you to be acceptable in their eyes? How much energy do you spend hiding from those around you? Do you have a secret life?

Compulsive overeating is a lonely disease. In our overeating careers all of us have done things which we're ashamed of, some related to food and some not. We've tried to cover up traces of binges and other negative behaviors so no one would know. The more we cover up, the more isolated we become.

What the OA program demands of us is rigorous honesty, and that is difficult if not impossible to achieve alone. We need the healing that comes from opening the dark corners of ourselves to another human being. Step Five requires courage—sometimes more than we think we have, until we remember that a Power greater than ourselves is leading and supporting us. That makes all the difference. We are not doing this alone. Help is available for the asking. Wanting to get well gives us courage.

How do you choose the person with whom to share your fifth Step? The most important criteria are that the person be someone with whom you are comfortable, that the person will understand what you are doing in Step Five, and that she or he can be trusted to protect your anonymity. This person may be a member of the clergy, a counselor, your sponsor or someone else in the program, a friend, or even a complete stranger. What counts is that this other human being be willing to receive you just as you are, the good and the bad.

If you haven't already completed your inventory, one way to motivate yourself is to make a definite appointment with the person you choose for Step Five. You may be reluctant to call someone and request help. Ask yourself if you are reluctant because you are shy or because you are proud. If being completely honest with God and ourselves requires humility, revealing ourselves to another person requires even more. When we decide we cannot afford to be too proud to ask for help, we are heading for recovery.

Experience has taught us we cannot live alone with our pressing problems and the character defects which cause or aggravate them. If Step Four has revealed in stark relief those experiences we'd rather not remember, then the need to quit living by ourselves with those tormenting ghosts of yesterday gets more urgent than ever. We have to talk to somebody about them. (Twelve and Twelve, p. 56)

Exactly the Way It Is

I can't tell anyone that I stole money out of my mother's purse to buy candy when I was a child . . . that I slept with my boss in order to get a promotion . . . that I can't be in the same room with my son for fifteen minutes without yelling at him . . . that I hide boxes of junk food on my closet shelf . . . that the reason I took a job in another city and relocated my family was to get away from all the lies I had told . . . that the reason I didn't go to an important social function last week was that none of my clothes fit and I was too gorged to move.

If you have chosen a sympathetic, understanding person who has had some experience with life and with people, it is unlikely that anything you say will come as an overwhelming shock to him or her. Probably your confidant will be honored to share something so important to you. Most likely the person will react to your sincerity and honesty with a great deal of respect and a genuine desire to help.

How would you feel if someone asked a similar favor of you? Do you think you are head and shoulders above everyone else in your willingness to be helpful? If you have chosen to share your inventory with another member of the program, the experience will undoubtedly be as beneficial to that person as it is to you. That's the way this program works—we can't keep the benefits we receive unless we give them away.

Holding back what you feel is too embarrassing to reveal will only detract from the cleansing process and the sense of peace that you want to experience. If you deal only in vague generalities such as "I've always been afraid" or "I get mad easily," you are glossing over the exact incidents that have made you feel guilty. Be specific. You may not want to share some of your personal problems with family members and others close to you. But here you are with an understanding listener, one you trust to protect your anonymity. Now is your chance. You are not trying to impress the other person; you are working for recovery.

You may wish to read your inventory just as you have written it, or you may want to expand and fill in details. If your listener is familiar with the program, he or she might suggest beginning the session with a short prayer. Those who have already taken the fourth and fifth Steps will perhaps want to share parts of their own inventories or relate to your experience with some of theirs. Whatever happens, chances are you will feel much better when you leave the session than when you came. Remember, the more specific and exact you are, the more freedom you will know when you have "given away" your inventory.

Like the rest of the program, the fifth Step works. The psychological and spiritual value of confession has been demonstrated for centuries. In the Twelve Step program, we take advantage of a proven method of enhancing emotional health and spiritual well-being. More than that, the ability to be honest with ourselves, God, and our fellow human beings has become crucially important for those of us who seek recovery from compulsive overeating.

Often we discover that what had seemed so shameful in our own minds is not that grim when exposed to the light of day and a "sympathetic other." Mistakes from the past are particularly apt to get blown out of proportion simply because we have kept them to ourselves. No matter what we have or have not done, the past is over and can be forgiven. By telling our story truthfully, we can lay to rest "those tormenting ghosts of yesterday."

Join the Human Race

Part of the necessary ego-reduction we must go through in order to recover from our illness is to accept the fact that we are human and therefore make mistakes. Since a compulsive overeater is often a perfectionist, such acceptance is not easy. Trying to do things perfectly can apply to anything from a food plan to writing a report to cleaning a house. The harder we try, the more anxiety we experience. When we do make an error, we use that as an excuse to hate ourselves and to stop trying. How is a compulsive overeater tempted to relieve anxiety and self-hate? By overeating, of course.

In Step Five, we say to our Higher Power, to ourselves, and to another person, "All right, I'm not perfect. And here is some of the evidence." We become willing to present ourselves as we are without hiding the blemishes. Instead of trying to maintain an image of superiority, we analyze our weaknesses so we can make constructive changes. Usually our listener can help us see that our image of superiority was unnecessary in the first place and that it only got in our way. No one can avoid making mistakes. So why be miserable attempting to do the impossible?

Of course you're not perfect. Who is? Why not join the human race, and together let's see what we can do about acknowledging ourselves as we are right now. That is where we start. Any progress we make has to begin with what we are today.

Learning to Trust

With Step Five we begin to remove the walls we have created between ourselves and other people. It has been said that we can only know as much of ourselves as we are willing to reveal to someone else. But in order to be willing to reveal ourselves, we need to trust the other person. If in the past you have been afraid that people would let you down, you may have decided to go it alone—to depend only on yourself. How well has that worked?

Experience has demonstrated that until we come out of the self-imposed emotional isolation that often goes along with compulsive overeating, we do not recover. It is not only our eating habits that have gone awry; our interpersonal relationships often leave us unfulfilled and empty. Coming to this program is an admission that we are sick and tired of trying to go it alone. However frightening it may be to trust someone else to help us, it is worse to continue down the path of solitary self-destruction. Through the program, we are led to people we *can* trust and to friends who do not let us down.

For a variety of reasons, many of us have become very good at hiding from other people. (A favorite hiding place for a compulsive overeater is, of course, the refrigerator.) Coming out of hiding goes hand in hand with developing a sense of trust. One is not possible without the other. We do not learn to trust a Higher Power, ourselves, and other people until we stop hiding, and we only stop hiding as we develop enough confidence to reveal who we really are. It happens little by little. Trusting another person with our inner selves does not stop with the fifth Step; it continues throughout our recovery.

We come to this program and hear other people talk who have had experiences similar to ours. We can relate to what they say, and we can relate to them as fellow compulsive overeaters and fellow human beings. We feel at home. We begin to share our own experiences and find that people don't laugh or think we're crazy. They understand. It feels good to be able to talk about what we tried to hide, and it helps to get feedback from empathetic friends.

So we begin to reach out, to reveal a little more about ourselves, to trust an ever-widening circle of people. After all, what have we got to lose? OA says that if we don't like the program, our misery will be cheerfully refunded. How can we withhold trust from those who have been through the same sort of hell that we have and who sincerely want to help? Sharing our inventories is a giant step toward learning to trust other people. We gain a new sense of belonging and relatedness. We're less alone. The world becomes less fearful.

Communicating

After fully revealing yourself to another person in Step Five, you will find more freedom to be honest and open in other relationships, too. The dark secrets are off your chest. You don't have to hide and cover up any more. Self-respect soars with the feeling of having nothing to conceal.

The desire to communicate is one of our deepest cravings. As children we are relatively candid and spontaneous in the way we express ourselves, and we talk about what is important to us. As we grow older, we become more wary of expressing how we really feel. We become afraid to say things that might upset an important relationship. Instead, we tell the people we love what we think they want to hear.

In our interactions with other people, we may build up defenses so no one will be able to see through the image we are attempting to project. Defending an image is solitary business. It leads to superficial conversation, which fails to satisfy our need to relate to others on a meaningful level. If we are trying to present an image of how we think we should be—cool, sophisticated, tough, smart, gracious, or whatever—we are relating in an artificial way. The image isn't real, so the communication doesn't satisfy.

Lacking the warmth of genuine interaction with the important people in our lives, those of us who are compulsive overeaters turn to food to fill the emptiness. As our defenses build, pride prevents us from reaching out to other people. "I don't need anyone. I can be self-sufficient. I can take care of myself." We pretend that everything is fine—all we need to do is lose a few pounds. What problems we have are someone else's fault. We will not display any hint of weakness, because that would threaten the image we have carefully worked to create.

If we only tell people the good things, we are trying to live a lie. What's worse, we cut ourselves off from feedback and from outside help to deal with life's gut-level difficulties.

There is the possibility of going to the other extreme and pouring out never-ending tales of woe. That doesn't make for satisfying communication either. Even though we will probably do most of the talking in our fifth Step, we will also listen carefully to our listener's reaction.

Going over our inventories and our stories with someone else gives us the benefit of a fresh perspective and another person's experience. We don't have to keep trying to sort out the problems alone. An honest response to what we have to share increases our self-knowledge and confidence. Even an attitude of quiet listening conveys understanding and acceptance to us. Through Step Five we become more open to the possibility of genuine communication. We learn from the insights of others, and our hunger for genuine communication is satisfied.

Toward Recovery

Our journey toward recovery continues. When we share our inventories and those experiences and feelings that have troubled us most, we come out of isolation. We make a breakthrough toward improved relationships with other people. These relationships will eventually provide us with the kind of emotional nourishment that food never did and never will. Cleansing and healing take place, opening the way for further emotional and spiritual growth.

Many who have taken Step Five report that they experience the love, acceptance, and forgiveness of a Higher Power in a tangible way. Like many other experiences in the program, this gift from a Higher Power is often mediated through another person. When we feel the love and acceptance of another human being who knows "the worst" about us, simultaneously we can feel the forgiveness of our Higher Power. This sets us free to be who we are.

Sometimes the experience is described as one of rebirth. It is as though the past has been laid to rest and a new beginning made possible. We get rid of some of the emotional roadblocks—especially guilt and fear. Then we are able to move on. This may mean finally having the courage to go back to school, to look for a new job, to extricate ourselves from damaging relationships, to make positive commitments. The healing that comes with this Step can give us a fresh perspective on how we want to spend the rest of our lives, one day at a time.

Most important, we are continuing to grow spiritually. A Higher Power is here with us when we acknowledge our need for him. We admit our weaknesses and our failures, and we are given strength to try again, this time with new insight and new faith. The fifth Step is not something we do once and for all. It's an ongoing process. As we develop and change, we will probably want to make periodic inventories to evaluate our progress. Each time we share them, we get rid of more debris and make new, positive discoveries.

As we move through the Steps toward recovery, we are moving into freedom. Freedom from food abuse and the self-destructive habit of overeating is what we were desperately seeking when we came to this program. But we find more. We find forgiveness and love. We find new possibilities for handling difficult situations constructively.

There may be an actual physical sensation of relief and lightness after taking Step Five. There will also be progress toward the emotional freedom and self-knowledge that makes it possible to maintain abstinence. With the fifth Step we take another stride toward closer relationships with our fellow human beings and toward the spiritual freedom that comes from daily surrender to a Power greater than ourselves.

Step Six

GETTING READY TO LET GO

Were entirely ready to have God remove all these defects of character.

In Step Six we are preparing ourselves for the action of a Higher Power. We are getting ready, "entirely ready to have God remove all these defects of character" (Big Book, p. 59). The accent is on what we believe a Higher Power can do, provided we are willing to let go of our liabilities and follow the directions for recovery.

Through the first five Steps we have come to the realization that we are not able to be what we want to be without effective outside help. This is not just another self-improvement project. Most of us have spent lots of time—usually many years—trying to improve ourselves one way or another. When we embrace the Overeaters Anonymous program, we do so because everything else has failed to yield permanent results. The sixth Step further amplifies what the program is all about: surrendering our own wills, being open to the action of a Higher Power, and cooperating with that Higher Power's will for our lives.

Your first reaction to Step Six may be to say, "That's easy. Of course I'm ready to have my character defects removed. They're all yours, H.P. Take them away." However, the apparent easiness of this Step may be deceptive. As with so many other aspects of an overeaters program, being ready is simple, yes—but easy, no.

Shakespeare said that "ripeness is all." Certainly the Twelve Step program is something we can absorb only as we become ready to receive it. Some of us are not ready when we are first introduced to OA. "Not for me," we say. Then we continue to bungle along doing things *our* way until the situation becomes so intolerable that even what we didn't like about OA begins to make some sense. Then we may be willing to go back to a meeting and listen again.

We start to take the Steps, but we can only move along as we become ready. Sometimes progress seems painfully slow. It may seem to us that we're going backward instead of forward. Sometimes we do need to back up and retake one or more Steps. Perhaps we didn't do a thorough enough job the first time. Perhaps we've changed and developed, and we're more aware of what is going on inside our heads. Taking the Twelve Steps is not something we do once and for all. It is the work of a lifetime. We can always go deeper and learn more.

If we have honestly come to terms with our character defects, we see that we have had them for a long time in spite of our efforts to "reform." We are unable to pull them out like weeds. As we become more aware of what our Higher Power has done and continues to do for us, it begins to make sense that if our liabilities are going to be exchanged for assets, it will be by the grace of God rather than by our own efforts alone.

But being ready to have our defects removed means being willing to give them up, to live without them. Although we deplore our limitations and weaknesses, we may also be emotionally and physically attached to them. "Make me pure, Lord, but not yet," the old saying goes. We need to arrive at a state where we are convinced that the pain of hanging on to our defects is greater than the pain of letting them go.

Sometimes this state of readiness is slow in coming. As long as we harbor the possibility of a softer, easier way to recover from compulsive overeating, we are not ready. As long as we cling to the illusion of our own self-sufficiency, we are not ready. As long as we are afraid to depend on the wisdom and the timing of a Higher Power, we are not ready.

Being ready means that we have exhausted the other options and possibilities. We become willing to let go of the physical craving and mental obsession that compels us to overeat. We are also willing to let a Higher Power guide us away from the defects that keep us from living useful, loving lives, those same defects that drive us back to using excess food to fulfill our emotional and spiritual needs. Our role is to loosen our grasp on the spurious rewards of false pride, fear, selfishness, anger, envy, and everything else that stands in the way of recovery and serenity.

While we remember that we have not been able to replace our liabilities with assets by ourselves, we become open to the action of a Higher Power. If we refuse to let go of our defects, we're like children who want their broken toys repaired but won't give them up to be fixed. Are we ready?

Willing to Change

If we ask, God will certainly forgive our derelictions. But in no case does He render us white as snow and keep us that way without our cooperation. That is something we are supposed to be willing to work toward ourselves. He asks only that we try as best we know how to make progress in the building of character. (Twelve and Twelve, p. 66)

Growth is not possible unless we are willing to move away from old habits, which have the ease of familiarity despite the pain they cause. If we continue to head straight for the refrigerator every time we get home from work, we will very likely activate the habit of compulsive overeating. We become attached to our habits. It feels more secure to stay with them than to carry out a new course of action. But now that we are letting our lives be managed by a Higher Power, we can follow God's guidance to new ways of acting. Step Six requires our willingness to change and to be guided.

If you consistently get angry while talking to your Aunt Mabel and then binge afterwards, there are several possibilities for doing things differently. You can stop talking to your Aunt Mabel. You can vent your anger by punching a pillow or taking a brisk walk instead of eating. You can come to the realization that your anger is doing more damage to you than to Aunt Mabel, and you can decide to relinquish the anger by letting God remove it.

If we are going to recover from compulsive overeating, it's certain that our ways of feeling and acting need to be altered. The old ways have led us to a state of desperation. We become aware that our illness is a progressive one, and that's strong motivation to try something new and different. If we do not change, we are in danger of taking years off our life spans and adding mountains of misery to the years we do have. It makes a good deal of sense to stop clinging to old, familiar, self-destructive habits.

Letting a Higher Power remove the obstacles to our recovery is not a passive procedure but one requiring our active collaboration. Not only do we need an attitude of willingness, but we also have to do the kind of footwork that will bring us, physically and mentally, to a place where we are receptive to God's action. Going to meetings, reading the literature, talking to other OA members, thinking of ways to reorganize our activities so that we avoid what we know we can't handle, is evidence of our willingness to change. Concentrating on the positive characteristics we want to develop, such as courage, serenity, gratitude, and confidence, points us in the right direction.

Old habits die hard. We are dealing with attitudes, feelings, and behavior that have become ingrained over a long period of time. When progress with the sixth Step seems slow, ask yourself what you could be doing to become more available and open to the guidance of a Higher Power. If you have come to believe that God works through other people, you will stay close to those who are living examples of the program's success.

In some areas of the country, there are OA meetings every day. If you are lucky enough to be in one of those locations, how about taking advantage of more meetings? Perhaps you can organize a new group. If it requires a meeting every day to keep you in a new frame of mind and working the program, then do that for as long as you need to in order to form new habits. Giving recovery top priority on your daily schedule is further evidence of your willingness to do things differently.

Immersing ourselves in a recovery program for overeaters opens us to change in several ways. Initially, we find something besides eating that will fill our spare time. Becoming active in an overeaters program, giving service, and following a plan for personal development are all constructive activities that foster emotional and spiritual growth. Most of us need to get out of our isolated ruts and interact more with other people. A program gives us that opportunity, if we are willing to take it. Being open to change might reveal itself in an act as simple – and sometimes as difficult – as moving the body out of the kitchen.

Then there's the change in attitude that comes with working the Steps. We are gradually turned from being self-centered to being centered in a Higher Power. We may not be able to explain this change or put our finger on exactly what has happened, but *something* has happened. Before now, we thought we had to maintain tight control over ourselves and our lives. Now we can relax with a growing confidence that whatever occurs will be okay. A Higher Power is in charge. Whether the change in attitude comes about by our seeing examples of how a program has worked for other people or by our experiencing firsthand God's action in our lives, something new has happened to us. And it transforms our ways of thinking and behaving.

Don't fight it. Step Six is a further example of a Higher Power doing for us what we cannot do for ourselves. Little by little we become willing to grow spiritually. One of the most effective means of encouraging this rewarding development is to take time for meditation every day. This may include reading from one of the Twelve Step meditation books. As this becomes a habit that we perform whether or not we "feel like it," we broaden the channel for God's action and for positive change. If there are still some defects that we are not ready to have removed, we can pray for willingness. We can ask to be given more faith. We can ask to be more loving and understanding. And we can act as if we already possess these assets.

Why Me?

One of the biggest and most stubborn roadblocks to being entirely ready to exchange our weaknesses for strengths in Step Six is the nagging feeling of resentment, the self-pitying attitude of Why me? Why did I have to be a compulsive overeater? Why did I get saddled with all these quirks and personality problems? Why can't I eat like normal people? Why can't I manage my own life?

Accepting ourselves as we are right now is a prerequisite for change and progress. Why am I a compulsive overeater? Who knows? Blaming my mother, my early environment, my spouse, my job or lack of one is counterproductive. I might just as well ask myself why I am nearsighted, why I have headaches, or why I am allergic to grass. Everyone has disabilities in one form or another. The sooner we can accept the fact that we are compulsive overeaters and need help with every area of our lives, the more effectively we can get on with the Steps to recovery.

Let's look at the positive side. We have an illness that can be controlled. Though it is serious and can be fatal if not treated, the means of control opens the door to an entirely new life. With abstinence and the Twelve Steps, we have a definite structure for growth. The process of recovery brings the kind of joy and peace we've never experienced before.

After a time in an overeaters' program, many of us begin to consider the craving to overeat as a sort of barometer indicating that something is wrong. If abstinence begins to get shaky, we realize that something is going on emotionally or spiritually that needs our attention. If it weren't for the problem of overeating, we might never be forced to face up to the character defects that exacerbate our problems.

Rather than resenting the fact that we are compulsive overeaters, we can become grateful for the good things that a program of recovery brings us. One of the best of these is fellowship. Perhaps for the first time in our lives, we have found a real sense of belonging and people who understand us. We can count on their support when we need it. Help during a time of temptation or despair or loneliness is only as far away as the telephone.

We do not have to resent being different from the people who were in our lives before we found an OA program. And now we have friends who can share the feelings and thoughts we used to conceal. Having the acceptance and understanding of a group of people who are working on the same problems that have plagued us helps us to understand and accept ourselves. This improves the way we relate to everyone around us, whether they're in the program or not.

Following the whims and dictates of self-will has helped perpetuate our compulsion. But our being convinced of the importance of maintaining abstinence from compulsive overeating doesn't guarantee that we will readily accept the idea of giving up control. We may still be tempted to indulge in a binge of self-pity, or an orgy of telling someone else what to do, or a fit of insisting on exactly what we want.

That won't work. If we give free rein to anger or self-pity, we find ourselves in the middle of an emotional storm or a mire of depression. If we persist in giving unsolicited advice or directions and orders that other people are not about to follow, we end up with a tremendous feeling of frustration. Pride and intransigence can wreck the most promising of relationships. And then, after indulging in these negative traits, where are we? At the very least we're deprived of serenity. And we're probably extremely upset and fighting the urge to overeat.

Serenity may seem boring at first glance. It is certainly not as exciting as riding an emotional roller coaster. And abstaining from emotional binges as well as from overeating binges leaves us with time to fill. But what we find is that the same Power that removes our defects leads us into constructive activities and fills us with a new sense of purpose and direction. When our emotional lives are on an even keel, we have the energy to accomplish useful projects and be of service to other people. We have time to enjoy life instead of constantly being in the grips of negative emotions.

According to Step Six, when the pain generated by our liabilities becomes greater than the pleasure, and when our efforts at self-reform fail, we are ready for help from a Higher Power. Why me? Why am I in this mess? I may never find a satisfactory answer to these questions. But instead of resenting my predicament or indulging in self-pity, I can accept my need for God's help and ask God for the willingness to follow the directions for recovery.

No Finish Line

We know, of course, that we will never be rid of all our defects and liabilities. In an OA program there is no finish line. We will come back to Step Six many times. We are always learning, becoming, recovering. No one of us can say that he or she is completely recovered. We continue to be compulsive overeaters and unable to manage our lives without help from a Higher Power.

Did you first come to a program with the only purpose of losing weight? Most of us probably did. We thought that weight loss would solve all our problems. Then we realized that we were also suffering from an obsession that we could not control and that fueled our compulsive overeating behavior. Then we were told the paradox: we wouldn't gain control until we let go of it. We wouldn't be relieved of our physical compulsion or our mental obsession until we honestly came to terms with our character defects and became entirely ready to let go of them.

Many of us can testify that our obsession with food has gone. The craving with which we unsuccessfully struggled for longer than we care to remember has been lifted. With abstinence comes freedom from the constant preoccupation with what we are going to eat, how we are going to get it, how much we will consume. We are no longer ruled by "I shouldn't, I want, I won't, I will."

What surfaces when our obsession is removed? Often there is a great deal of pain, anger, fear, and anxiety that has been sublimated by the process of chewing and swallowing and focusing our attention on food. An overeaters' program provides us with tools for working on what is really bothering us and frees us from eating to try to make those unpleasant feelings disappear. We get valuable insights and help from other people in a program, and we build a spiritual relationship with a Higher Power.

Once we have turned our will and our lives over to the God of our understanding, the specifics of how and when improvement comes are up to the Higher Power. We don't set up a schedule for the elimination of our problems by taking Step Six. We may have to live with some of our problems for an indefinite period of time. Step Six gets us ready to follow inner promptings as they come to us and to try sincerely to determine our Higher Power's will for us just for today. What we can do is focus on becoming completely willing to surrender our false pride, our fear, our self-sabotaging reactions whenever they appear. We can work to establish genuine relationships of mutual give and take. They will nourish us in a way that excess food never did. This takes time, but so did compulsive overeating.

We are putting ourselves in the hands of a Higher Power, and we are asking for new attitudes and new ways of responding to problems. The answers will come, and the results may surprise us. Inner changes may occur that we never would have believed possible. When we look back, we may see that some event or growth in understanding had to take place before we could be freed from a particular problem or defect of character. As we develop trust that a Higher Power is guiding us, we learn how to cooperate more patiently with the unfolding of our lives.

Our liabilities are removed when we are ready to let go of them. New areas that need work are revealed as we are able to handle them. Since we are never going to be finished, we need to concentrate on living one day at a time and be satisfied with slow improvement. This is the state of readiness described in the sixth Step.

Because home, school, and society have taught us to be goal oriented, living one day at a time takes practice. We compulsive people have been deluded by the idea that one day we will cross some magic finish line and everything will be wonderful. Many of us used to drive ourselves obsessively to attain our goals, seeking the nirvana that the finish line was supposed to produce.

For compulsive people, nirvana never comes. It is always in the next bite or the next accomplishment. It's not that we don't need goals. We do. What an overeaters' program suggests is that we make our plans but leave the results to God. That way we don't focus anxiously on goals to the point that we're unable to enjoy life right now. Half the fun of future goals is getting to them ... maybe more than half.

As long as we are alive, there is no finish line. When we reach one goal, another lies ahead. This is good. It means that we keep growing. We would like to be perfect right now, but that's not the way life works. The thing to remember is that we are seeking progress in the building of character, not perfection. By cooperating with our Higher Power, we become entirely ready to let go of our defects and continue the process of recovery.

LET GO AND LET GOD

Humbly asked Him to remove our shortcomings.

Do you believe that the God of your understanding created you to be compulsive or that God created you to be free? Discovering the freedom that comes with turning one's will and life over to the care of a Higher Power is the Step by Step adventure of the Overeaters Anonymous program.

Coming to Step Seven, we find ourselves again in a direct relationship with this Higher Power. We are asking God to remove our shortcomings — everything that is standing in the way of our freedom to develop our potential fully. In Step Six we spent as much time as was necessary to become ready to make this request wholeheartedly. Now we are making it, humbly and sincerely, believing that we are meant to have the freedom of recovery.

The Big Book of Alcoholics Anonymous gives the following seventh Step prayer:

My Creator, I am now willing that you should have all of me, good and bad. I pray that you remove from me every single defect of character which stands in the way of my usefulness to you and my fellows. Grant me strength, as I go out from here, to do your bidding. Amen. (Big Book, p. 76)

By this time, we are well aware of what a mixed bag we are giving our Higher Power when we give ourselves. We say, "You can have me, God, defects and all. I want you to sort me out, to take away what needs to be eliminated and to make me useful to you and the people around me." As we give ourselves to God, we seek to have fewer liabilities and more assets.

Do you find it hard to ask for what you want? Do you expect to be given what you would like to have without the necessity of asking for it? Are you afraid to ask for fear the answer might be no? Are you too proud to ask for what you need? (If you believe that God, if asked, *will* remove your defects, and this is what's frightening you, then you may need to go back to Step Six. You may not be entirely ready.)

Assuming we are prepared to "talk turkey," let's examine the attitude we need to have in order to humbly ask God to remove our shortcomings.

Asking God to do this implies that the matter is out of our control. Most of us compulsive overeaters have tended to *demand* things from life, from God, from other people, and from ourselves. When these demands have not been met, we have raged, sulked, complained, retaliated, or given up. Asking is not demanding. Asking God implies a dialogue, not a self-centered soliloquy. When we ask, we leave ourselves vulnerable to the response of our Higher Power. And it may not come in the way we expect or desire or think is best.

To ask God for help is to concede that we are unable to accomplish what we want by ourselves. We are not self-sufficient. The process of our ego reduction continues. Self-will may kick and scream with varying degrees of intensity. If we are headstrong and like to feel independent, it goes against the grain to ask for anything. For example, some of us may drive miles out of our way because we are reluctant to stop and ask for directions. Any admission of ignorance seems an indication of weakness. How many times have we tried to bluff our way through something because we were too embarrassed to admit that we didn't know how to do it?

But the moment comes when we run out of time and patience. Perhaps after all our bright ideas for fixing the leaky faucet fail, we finally call the plumber before we end up with a flood. The pain we tried to eliminate with various home remedies gets worse, so we finally go to the doctor. Similarly, when we get sufficiently tired and sore from beating our heads against the brick wall of our character defects, we ask God please to get them out of our way.

Our prayer may go like this: "I don't know as much as I thought I did, God. I thought if I stopped overeating and got thin, all my problems would disappear along with the fat, and I would live happily ever after. I thought if I could just get my husband or wife or child to a psychiatrist, everything would be fine. I thought having enough money would be the answer, but there's never enough. I thought a new job would make life exciting, but I'm still bored."

External changes do not alter the fact that we still have to live with our inner selves. If we are not in harmony with our own needs, circumstances will never suit us, no matter how we try to rearrange them.

"I'm the one who has to change, God. I'm asking You to show me how."

But Who Wants to Be Humble?

When we were overeating compulsively, humility may not have seemed relevant or desirable. The word humility itself may have sounded old-fashioned and naive, fine for saints but impractical in the real world. Many of us grew up oriented to achievement and self-sufficiency rather than to dependence on a Higher Power and obedience to his will.

We didn't want to be humble; we wanted to be high. We ate what we wanted, when we wanted, and as much as we wanted. This was our way of demonstrating our control over life. Nothing was going to come between us and our satisfaction.

The problem was, it didn't work. The high soon turned into a low, as did the other highs we tried—alcohol, drugs, ego trips, and selfish sex, to name a few. Using food to feel high made most of us fat, and even if we were able to avoid the fat, the binges left us depressed and full of self-hate.

The old adage that pride goes before a fall has proved itself countless times in our overeating careers. We think everything is going great. We finally have the situation in hand. We forget that we are compulsive overeaters, and we go slipping right down into a binge. After that, we are very, very low.

Humility may not sound appealing, but experience demonstrates that it is the necessary precondition for recovery. For many of us, admitting that we are powerless over food is the beginning of humility. Much as we have tried to prove that we are not really powerless over food ("Maybe I'm only powerless over certain foods . . . powerless at certain times . . . powerless under certain conditions . . ."), we finally admit that we are—period.

By allowing us to recognize our inability to control what we eat once we take the first compulsive bite, humility makes physical abstinence possible. By allowing us to recognize a similar inability to control our character defects by ourselves, humility creates the kind of spiritual condition in which a Higher Power can work with us and through us. If we allow pride to take over, we fall back into the illusion that we are in control. And we fail every time—physically, emotionally, and spiritually. We may not *like* the idea of being humble, but there is no other way. We will keep getting beaten down by pride until we become humble enough to ask for help and listen to the answer. Like water, humility seeks the lowest level and then, paradoxically, becomes a source of strength and nourishment. When we are humble, we are open to a Higher Power that can do for us what self-will cannot.

Each day, one day at a time, we are given a reprieve from our illness. To have this reprieve, it is necessary to maintain the spiritual condition of humility. Then the character defects can be defused. They may never disappear entirely. Like the urge to overeat, the potential remains. But those character defects can remain inactive as long as we are focused on letting a Higher Power govern us, and as long as we do not go back to trying to control our own lives and the lives of others.

Step Seven is a continuation of Step Six. We have become ready to have our character defects removed because we are sick and tired of the chaos they produce in our lives and the lives of those around us. We are asking a Higher Power to remove our shortcomings, and the only way we can communicate with this Higher Power is by asking humbly. Then, in order to have the defects removed, we need to be humble enough to learn new attitudes and new ways of acting.

One definition of humility is "being teachable." We don't have to wear sackcloth and ashes to be humble, and we don't have to feel inferior. (We are not alone in having defects of character.) Being humble simply means having a realistic view of ourselves that allows us to grow and learn. If we accept the fact that we don't know everything, then we will not be locked into self-destructive patterns of behavior. We can be willing to change if we are not rigid with pride. If we are humble, we will not be afraid to try something new. It is pride that insists on always being right and always having the answers.

Step Seven's prerequisite is humility. Without it, we do not recognize the shortcomings that damage us and others. It takes humility to ask a Higher Power to remove them instead of continuing to try to cope with them in a habitually headstrong way. We cannot demand to have the defects removed. We have to be humble enough to ask. So it is that humility becomes desirable when we see it as a key to our recovery.

Indeed, the attainment of greater humility is the foundation principle of each of [OA's] Twelve Steps. For without some degree of humility, no [compulsive overeater] can stay [abstinent] at all. Nearly all [participants in OA] have found, too, that unless they develop much more of this precious quality than may be required just for [abstinence], they still haven't much chance of becoming truly happy. Without it, they cannot live to much useful purpose, or, in adversity, be able to summon the faith that can meet any emergency. (Twelve and Twelve, p. 71)

Our Shortcomings

Everyone has character defects, but the only ones we ask God to remove are our own. One of the reasons overeaters' programs work is that they teach us to concentrate on how to change our own thinking and behavior rather than how we might be able to manipulate and control other people. If we let someone else's behavior destroy our emotional equilibrium, we are in trouble, since we are powerless to change that person. What we can do is accept the responsibility for our own reactions and learn how to change them. If we react with anger or pain to what someone else says or does, that is our problem. We own our reactions. That means we can choose to let go of the ones that hurt us.

Over the course of the years, we have probably blamed our compulsive overeating on everybody and everything outside of ourselves. "I was the youngest child in the family and was always rewarded with sweets." "My father didn't love me enough." "I was insecure." "We moved constantly, and I didn't have any real friends." "My job is boring and frustrating." "My wife has lost interest in sex, and so I eat." "My son has dropped out of school." "My mother-in-law came to live with us." "I'm going through a divorce." All marvelous reasons for overeating—or so we rationalize.

However, if we recall our past objectively, we see that there was *always* a "reason" for overeating and that if it hadn't been one thing, it would have been another. But in fact we overate because we were compulsive overeaters. The deeper we get into the Steps, the more clearly we understand that our various problems did not cause us to overeat. Often it was the other way around: *our overeating created unnecessary problems*. We sought in food what we could not realistically expect from life—the satisfaction of all our impulses and desires.

Because we were hooked on overeating, we withdrew from people and retreated into self-centered fear and pride. Grandiosity and ignorance prompted us to think the answer was *more*—more food, money, sex, power—you name it. But trying to get more and more didn't work. In Step Seven we are asking a Higher Power to take over our lives and remove the shortcomings that prevent us from being of service to God and to our fellow human beings. We're talking about *our* shortcomings. Not our boyfriend's laziness or our boss's temper, but *our* tendency to procrastinate and *our* self-righteous anger.

Often, the characteristics that annoy us about other people are the very same weaknesses we would rather not recognize in ourselves. We project our own shortcomings and see them as someone else's character defects. For example, we tend to be most critical of our children when we see in them some of the same negative traits that we ourselves exhibit.

If we delude ourselves into thinking that our recovery depends on the behavior of the people with whom we live or the external circumstances and events that affect our lives, we are putting ourselves in a bind. People and circumstances will never suit us perfectly. But we don't have to use that as an excuse to overeat or to hang on to our own defects of character. Serenity and sanity come to us not when other people do what we want them to do but when our first priority is to try sincerely to know and do God's will for us.

Growing Pains

We ask God to remove the obsession with food over which we are powerless, and then we consider abstinence to be a gift from our Higher Power. For some of us, abstinence may come with relative ease once we completely surrender to the fact that when we take the first compulsive bite we are truly powerless over food. We come to accept that in order to grow up, we have to stop using excess food as a crutch. For others of us, abstinence may hurt for a while as our self-will and habits still struggle to retain control. (Self-will can masquerade as hunger, fatigue, fear, or any other rationale we use to prove that we are not compulsive overeaters.)

If we have to be uncomfortable for a period of time in order to learn how to face life without overeating, then so be it. The long-term freedom is well worth some temporary pain. Remember, none of us would choose to stay with an overeaters' program if the pain of overeating were not far worse than whatever initial discomfort abstinence involved.

When we let go of our obsession with food, we begin to experience the peace and joy of being free from the compulsion to eat more and more. Humility is the key. As we become increasingly aware of the liabilities we have in addition to compulsive overeating, we use the same seventh Step key to open ourselves to the Higher Power, so that we may be freed from these shortcomings as well. But here, too, the process of growth may involve some short-term discomfort.

Our growing pains may be experienced as a series of waves that can, like ocean waves, overwhelm us with their immensity and power. By maintaining contact with our Higher Power, we learn to ride most of the waves. Every so often, one of the big ones may temporarily submerge us. But we know that it, too, will pass. The wave may knock us down. But through the program we are developing an inner core of peace that keeps us from being destroyed by fear or confusion.

When we tried to anesthetize ourselves with food to keep from feeling pain, our emotional and spiritual growth was arrested. God does not insulate us from hurt. Sometimes we have to feel pain in order to get better. What our Higher Power does is provide us with enough strength, faith, and inner peace to be able to roll with the punches and to learn the lessons contained in the unpleasant experiences. Pain is a teacher. It is a warning signal that we are off the track.

Like a splinter that needs to be removed or a tooth that needs to be pulled, our defects need to go. If we put our Higher Power in charge of recovery, we can recognize the pain of growth and know that it will not destroy us. In fact, growing pains are part of getting better.

Service

In the seventh Step prayer quoted earlier, we asked God to remove our defects so that we could not only be free of them but also be useful to God and to our fellow human beings. When we were compulsively overeating, we were wrapped up in ourselves. Food was our god, and the idea of service was not a priority. This is changing. As we live the new freedom and enthusiasm of abstinence, our gratitude for such a priceless gift makes us want to give in return.

The new life into which we are growing is not self-centered. The more firmly we are grounded in a Higher Power, the better we feel and the more we want to be useful. We have learned that striving for material satisfaction does not work as a primary goal. We are discovering that happiness comes as a by-product of seeking to know and follow God's will for our lives. We are not going to be perfect, but we can give to other people in spite of that. When we humbly put a Higher Power in charge of our renovation, we can relax and stop beating ourselves for our faults. God made us and is remaking us every day—and God doesn't make mistakes.

One of the reasons we were seeking the answer to life's questions in the refrigerator undoubtedly was that we had no workable, day-to-day, gut-level faith in a Power greater than ourselves. We may have believed in God, but we did not concretely apply that belief to our everyday thoughts and actions.

Now we are linked to a Power that makes a practical, fundamental difference in both the trivial and the significant events in our lives. We have found the strength and inspiration of an overeaters' group, and the love and support of understanding individuals who want our strength, hope, and love. An important part of our usefulness to God and our fellow human beings is what we give back to our group and what we share with family and friends outside the program.

Step Seven points the way to the freedom to be and do the best we can. The more we let ourselves be filled with the gifts our Higher Power has for us each day, the less room there will be for character defects. We pray simply and humbly for their removal. Then we can go about the business of the day, relying on God's grace to guide us, to fill our lives, and to overflow to those around us.

Step Eight

GETTING HONEST

Made a list of all persons we had harmed, and became willing to make amends to them all.

In Step Eight our job is to list the people we have harmed and to become willing to make amends to all of them. Although many of us might like to skip this Step, it is an integral part of a program of recovery for compulsive overeaters. It enables us to maintain abstinence and serenity and to grow emotionally and spiritually.

In the *Twelve Steps and Twelve Traditions*, "harm" is described as "the result of instincts in collision which cause physical, mental, emotional, or spiritual damage to people" (Twelve and Twelve, p. 80). Most of us can readily admit that our relationships with other people have not been as satisfying as they might be. Step Eight gives us the opportunity to go back over our past and identify those we have hurt by our actions and attitudes. Our goal is to repair, as best we can, the harm we have inflicted. Even if we feel that we are not yet willing to make amends to certain individuals, we can begin by making our list and praying that the willingness will come.

Since defective relations with other human beings have nearly always been the immediate cause of our woes, including our [compulsive overeating], no field of investigation could yield more satisfying and valuable rewards than this one. Calm, thoughtful reflection upon personal relations can deepen our insight. . . .Thoroughness, we have found, will pay—and pay handsomely. (Twelve and Twelve, p. 80)

If you followed the fourth Step guide in the Big Book, you may already have your list down in black and white. Most likely, the injured parties that first come to mind will be family members. We have more power to hurt those we love deeply than those who are casual acquaintances. Most of us have managed to do considerable damage to family and friends not only as a direct result of overeating, but also as a result of the character defects and liabilities we identified in Step Four.

It may be argued that compulsive overeaters do not lose control to the extent that they abuse their spouses, get arrested for reckless driving, or gamble away mortgage payments. However, what about the compulsive overeater who steals food? What about people who spend most of their time thinking about food, eating, and suffering from the effects of binges, rather than enjoying and helping other people? For a compulsive overeater, the sins of omission may be more glaring than the sins of commission.

When we are obsessed with food, interpersonal relationships are bound to be adversely affected. As food and eating become increasingly important, we withdraw from other people in order to eat without interruption or censure. Private binges become the favorite pastime of those of us who are closet eaters.

But after bingeing, we hate ourselves. The hate and anger spill over into all our dealings with others. A gorged parent screams at a child. A despairing teenager locks the door and refuses to talk to anyone. Spouses are sometimes ignored. Sometimes they're given an irrational, abusive tirade over a minor incident. Plans are canceled because the overeater is incapacitated. Work that needs to be done is neglected.

To say that a binge impairs normal functioning is a mild statement. Most of us can remember numerous examples of irrational behavior directly related to overeating. Some of us have lost jobs because of our compulsion. Some of us were literally eating our lives away, sinking deeper and deeper into boredom, apathy, and depression.

Since no one of us is completely isolated, our negative behavior inevitably affects other people. Let's examine our relationships with others. Whom have we harmed?

Some of the damage we have done to those around us may not appear to be related to compulsive overeating. But we still need to recognize any harm we have done and to become willing to make amends, whether the hurt is due directly to compulsive overeating or to basic character defects. This Step enables us to grow into a new state of freedom and peace.

Checking It Twice

Step Eight will seem unnecessarily difficult if we let our minds race ahead to figure out how we'll make amends. Restitution is the next step.

Right now, we are only concerned with writing our list and becoming willing to make amends to the people on it.

When we examine our relations with other people and recognize where we have inflicted harm, we also may be tempted to catalog the ways these people have hurt us. Probably there has been damage on both sides. But we are focusing only on the hurt *we* have caused. Our recovery does not depend on our recognizing the wrongs of others. It *does* depend on our acknowledging where we have been at fault.

If we begin to get defensive when we consider the problems we have had with people, we might remember that they may need our forgiveness just as much as we need theirs. But whether or not they recognize that need shouldn't affect our ability to forgive them. If we really want to straighten out our messed up relationships, we will try to let go of our resentments and forgive others. Then we can ask their forgiveness and find peace within ourselves.

The humility we are learning in an overeaters' program will ease our way into Step Eight. It is a great relief not to have to be right all the time. Becoming humble enough to admit our mistakes to others and ask their forgiveness frees us from a heavy burden of pride and guilt. We've all had problems with interpersonal relationships, and we all have regrets about lingering hard feelings. Now is our chance to begin to do what we can to promote healing.

One of the ingredients necessary for maintaining a solid, clean abstinence from compulsive overeating is honesty with ourselves and with others. If we have done devious things in the past, now is the time to plan our reparations. For example, have we blamed a brother or sister for the disappearance of food when we were responsible ourselves? Has compulsive overeating harmed family members in other ways? Were we too worn out from bingeing to pay attention to the needs of others?

As we look back over the past, do we find a long-standing feud with someone? In the light of this program, can we see our own part in contributing to the ill will? Have we insisted on trying to have everything our way? Have we tried to control other people's lives?

What about current relationships? As our resentments, self-pity, and unreasonable demands begin to fade, our vision clears. We can see our own role in creating trouble. Now that we are no longer hiding in the refrigerator and burying our heads in excess food, we have the time and energy to face what has gone wrong in our dealings with other people.

When we were overeating, we wanted to be left alone so we could overeat. When tension arose, our first thought was probably to escape into the comfort of food, our oldest and dearest friend. Since food was what we really depended upon, not people, we could be relatively unconcerned about the feelings of those around us. If they didn't like what we did to them, we could always eat.

The OA program gives us the opportunity to replace an unhealthy dependence on excess food with a healthy dependence on a Higher Power and interpersonal relationships. If our lives are going to be different in a positive way, we need to be fully aware of how we have contributed to strained or broken relationships in the past. We also need to be aware of any continuing tendencies to think of other people as objects that we can control, manipulate, or ignore, according to the whims of the moment. We won't change overnight. But we can be willing to take a hard look at our behavior and honestly try to see where we have acted in ways that sabotage relationships.

Instincts in Collision

As social animals we suffer from conflicts with other people. As recovering compulsive overeaters we need to thoroughly examine the patterns of our interactions with these important people in our lives to see where we have made mistakes. We are doing this for our own self-respect and emotional abstinence, as well as for mutual forgiveness and reconciliation.

If we are consumed with jealousy toward a sister and seize every chance to belittle her, she's hurt. And we feel bitter and small. We've asked God to remove our character defects. Now our job is to try to repair some of the damage they have done. So our sister goes onto the list, and we work on becoming willing to make amends to her and to build a better emotional climate between us.

Self-will run riot destroys the most promising of relationships. If we are involved in marital difficulties, we need to look at the role our compulsive overeating has played in creating them. Have we been generally bad-tempered because of our obsession with food and overeating? Have we avoided sex because too much food has made us feel uncomfortable and unattractive? Have we refused to participate in activities with our partners because we preferred to eat? Have we blown the family budget on food for ourselves? Are our partners ashamed of the way we look? Aside from the damage directly related to compulsive overeating, what harm have we done by letting our instincts and self-will tangle with those of our partners? In answering these questions, we discover other people to add to our Step Eight list.

Instincts collide within the family, and they collide on the job. Let's take a moment to examine our relationships with coworkers. Have we been critical and uncooperative? Have we engaged in malicious gossip? Have we stolen time from our employers by coming to work so exhausted from last night's binge that we could produce little or nothing all day? How has addiction to overeating interfered with our job performance? Have we harmed others in order to make ourselves look good or to get a promotion? If we have problems with coworkers, the only thing we can change is ourselves and our approach to the situation. We can start by acknowledging where we have been wrong and by adding the names of coworkers we have hurt to our Step Eight list.

If we really want relationships to improve, we will not sit and wait for the other person to do something to make it better. If trouble with other people is getting in the way of recovery from compulsive overeating, then it is up to us to make every effort to straighten out the tangled relationships. Becoming willing to make amends may be tough, but overeating out of resentment and hostility is worse.

As we work these Steps, we are growing spiritually. We are becoming able to think and act in ways we might have considered impossible at an earlier stage. Turning our wills and our lives over to the care of a Higher Power produces internal changes that, in turn, cause changes in our behavior. Earlier in our recovery, we might never have considered making the first move toward mending a broken or disintegrating relationship. Now that we are genuinely trying to know and do the will of our Higher Power, taking such a risk becomes possible. The question becomes how we think our Higher Power wants us to behave toward our fellow human beings, not what we think they may or may not deserve from us. When we accept responsibility for our part in the collision of instincts, we are moving toward healing and reconciliation.

What About Me?

In making the eighth Step list, we are first concerned with identifying everyone we have harmed, whether specifically because of overeating or because of character defects in general. Then the question arises, what about the harm we have done to ourselves? It is obvious that we have suffered from the effects of our compulsive behavior. Most of us were fat and miserable, often for a considerable length of time. Self-respect plummeted with every failure to solve the overeating problem. Anger and frustration were the outcome of trying to control the lives of other people. We need to become willing to make amends to ourselves as well.

The most effective amends we can make to ourselves for our physical, emotional, and spiritual suffering is our own recovery. Each hour of abstinence makes up for some of the bad times we have created through our overeating and character defects. The love and acceptance we find in an overeaters' program foster self-esteem and a growing conviction that our bodies, minds, and spirits deserve to be nurtured. What's more, our program provides the tools necessary for us to take care of ourselves on every level.

Recovery is seldom instantaneous. In order to accept the long-term discipline that is required, we need to be firmly convinced that we are worth the effort. Here is where a healthy self-love is important. When we like and respect ourselves, we're able to give to other people.

This is a selfish program in that our primary concern is to stop overeating. Until we do, we're unable to exercise our full potential for service to those around us. Maintaining abstinence may mean that we sometimes say no to someone else in order to keep from overeating.

Physical abstinence demonstrates the willingness to make amends to our bodies for the physical harm caused by compulsive overeating. Learning to let go of resentment, anger, fear, hate, self-pity, and all the other negative emotions prepares us to make amends to ourselves on the mental and spiritual levels. By becoming willing to let go of grievances against others, we are making amends to ourselves.

As we develop an attitude of forgiveness toward those who have harmed us, we can stop resenting them. By being willing to make amends to those we have hurt, we get rid of guilt and anger, two emotions that destroy our serenity. Making amends to ourselves is an inseparable part of making amends to those we have harmed.

Live and Let Live

In recognizing the harm we have done to other people, we begin to see situations from a less subjective point of view. We learn that recovery involves tolerating and understanding others rather than forcing them to be what we think they should be. We may come to understand, for the first time, how our obsession with food was perceived as rejection by our children. Now, instead of feeling annoyed at what formerly seemed to be their incessant demands for attention, we can more readily appreciate the legitimate needs of our children. We can also be more tolerant of the fact that a three-year-old cannot be expected to show much consideration for our need for privacy.

Instead of blaming our parents for everything that is wrong with us, in Step Eight we examine the possibility that we may have hurt them. As we look past our feelings and consider theirs, we may come to the conclusion that they did the best they could. Part of becoming willing to make amends is the ability to accept people, including ourselves, as we are. And, as a result, our lives become infinitely more serene.

So we're back to the fact that we cannot change anyone else, only ourselves. For example, the person with whom we live may have character traits we consider undesirable. If we love this person, we'll try to overlook the traits we don't like and concentrate on the ones we do like. When we can acknowledge what we have done to create interpersonal problems and when we sincerely want to make restitution, we open the channels for better communication and a more satisfying relationship. If we are willing to accept others as they are, we may find that our differences contribute to growth in a positive and complementary way.

When we were overeating, we probably felt as though everyone and everything was against us. Through the program, we find that we are not alone. The support we receive helps us to accept the world as it is, and the insight we gain increases our understanding of those around us.

Our growing ability to tolerate the foibles of others shouldn't come as a surprise. A Higher Power is now in charge of our lives, and anything is possible. We are not taking Step Eight on our own. We have come to believe that the God of our understanding is concerned with everything we do and is directing all the events of our lives. We know that we are unable to straighten out our tangled relationships without help, but we also know that help is available for the asking.

Gratefully Recovering

The eighth Step is an essential part of our recovery from compulsive overeating, since one aspect of the illness has been our inability to sustain the kind of warm and deep involvement with other people that provides emotional and spiritual nourishment. By becoming willing to do what we can to heal damaged and broken relationships, we are moving forward in recovery.

If you are having problems with this Step, don't forget that you have OA friends who can help. Sharing our uncertainties and questions will work better than trying to go it alone. A sponsor or someone else who has completed Step Eight will be able to listen with empathy and encouragement.

We are working the Twelve Steps carefully because we want to get well. If going back into the past and examining old hurts is sometimes painful, we accept the pain as part of our eventual healing. Since we now know that our physical and mental health requires us to be honest, particularly with ourselves, we can recognize and admit the harm we have done to other people, even if it hurts to face up to it. If false pride is an obstacle to recovery, then false pride has to go.

For abstinence and the other gifts of the overeaters' program, we are increasingly grateful. Each small incident of success in working the Steps gives us courage to risk turning a larger area of our lives over to the care of a Higher Power. We become so grateful to be recovering from compulsive overeating that we're willing to go to any lengths to maintain and promote that recovery, even if it means getting ready to swallow our pride, apologize, and make restitution for our mistakes.

We could spend the rest of our lives being miserable and waiting for others to make the first move toward reconciliation. Self-centered pride would have us do it that way. But the overeaters' program teaches us that there is a better way.

As we begin to recognize how we have been misguided by self-will, and as our old resentments are lifted, we acquire a genuine desire to make amends for past mistakes. We become ready to make amends by writing a list of the people we have harmed. And in Step Nine we begin to make amends to those we have listed.

BUILDING BRIDGES

Made direct amends to such people wherever possible, except when to do so would injure them or others.

The day of reckoning has come. Our lists are ready, and we're willing to begin making direct amends to all people we've harmed, whether or not the injury is related to compulsive overeating.

Step Nine is definitely an action Step, and a most important one. Conscientious and thorough execution of Step Nine is concrete evidence that we are living a program for overeaters, not merely paying lip service to it. In order to reap the full benefits that an overeaters' program offers, we have to "walk the walk" as well as "talk the talk."

According to the dictionary, amends are "something given or done to make up for injury, loss, or the like that one has caused." If we lose a book we borrowed from a friend, we make amends by replacing it with a new book. If we've gone on an eating binge and consumed our roommate's food, we apologize and replace the food.

Similarly, many of us overeaters have neglected our families because of an obsessive preoccupation with food and eating. In this case, making amends may be somewhat more complicated, but it's certainly not impossible. If we are entirely ready to take responsibility for our actions, and if we are relying on a Higher Power to help us change and make restitution, we will be given guidance and inner direction.

We've all done things that have made us feel ashamed and guilty. But instead of honestly facing the consequences of our actions, we've tried to obliterate the guilt and shame with more eating. Now that excess food is no longer an option, we have to find another way of dealing with skeletons in the closet.

Experience demonstrates that the people we've harmed often are more than willing to meet us halfway when we initiate an attempt to repair the relationship. Admitting where you have been wrong can prompt someone else to acknowledge his or her part in the difficulty. The hardest part is making that first move toward reconciliation. Even if the response from the injured person is not positive, we are moving toward our own recovery and greater peace of mind. What keeps us from getting discouraged is the conviction that a Higher Power is in charge, and that the outcome does not depend on the success or failure of our efforts. We do the best we can and leave the results to our Higher Power. Since we have turned over our wills and our lives, it's a no-lose situation. What we stand to lose is obsession with food, extra pounds, self-centered fear, and pride — all of which we can do without.

How do we make amends? That depends, of course, on the specific circumstances — the nature of the hurt and the people involved. It is safe to say that whatever shape the amends take, they will require honesty, courage, and the willingness to acknowledge our mistakes. Sponsors and friends from our overeaters' program can help. They will see the situation more objectively, and they can provide needed support.

Step Nine takes careful thought and preparation. Good judgment is necessary. No one should be injured anew as a result of the amends. We are not trying to relieve our own feelings of guilt at someone else's expense. For example, confessing infidelity to an unsuspecting partner is probably neither advisable nor justifiable, because of the damage and hurt that would result. We need to approach Step Nine prayerfully, seeking guidance from a Power greater than ourselves.

Saying "I'm Sorry"

Some of us find it painfully difficult to say, "I'm sorry." Others of us are quick to say the words but slow to show that we mean them. For those in the first category, let's think about how the process can become less painful.

Pride is usually the biggest stumbling block to a sincere apology. We become so ashamed and embarrassed about falling short of our own expectations and those of others that we want to sweep the damning evidence under the rug and pretend it never happened.

So long as we continue to labor under the delusion that we are or should be perfect, there is little room for an honest admission of error.

Fear enters into the picture, too. We may be convinced that if we admit our mistakes, everyone will discover how inadequate we really are. We are afraid of being humiliated. Apologizing leaves our tender, fragile egos exposed and vulnerable. But hard as it may be to swallow our pride and move beyond fear, it is more difficult to continue with a load of unresolved bad feelings, particularly if they involve people we see frequently or with whom we live.

Sometimes the apology needs to be made to someone who lives far away. It might have to be done by letter. Writing might be easier than a face-to-face encounter. However, if a personal meeting is possible, it is usually more effective.

Being willing to say "I'm sorry" means that we are moving beyond a self-centered point of view. We're learning to look at the situation from the other person's viewpoint. This is called empathy. It may have taken some of us a considerable amount of time to comprehend just how painful our words and actions have been to someone we love. But as we come to empathize, we will not be so concerned about our own pride and fear or the protection of our fragile egos.

Often we need to apologize not only for what we have done but also for what we have failed to do. As compulsive overeaters we've tended toward isolation. We may have frequently opted for eating rather than making an effort to do something with others.

Let's take a hypothetical example. Suppose a friend or family member has often suggested activities that could be enjoyed together. Suppose our response has usually been negative. This undoubtedly has hurt the other person's feelings and has stunted the growth of the relationship.

Perhaps as parents we've been unwilling to share our interests and energies with a child or teenager. Perhaps as wives or husbands we would rather watch television and eat than develop a joint hobby with our partners. Or maybe as a friend we have let the other person be responsible for making all the suggestions, and then we've usually vetoed them.

If we realize that our reluctance to give of ourselves has caused friction and bad feelings in our relationships, we can start to improve the situation by sitting down with the other person and expressing honest regret.

Perhaps the chaos created in our lives by compulsive overeating and character defects has not only strained our relationships but actually broken them. Being fired from a job, getting divorced, flunking out of school – these things can happen. And on sane and sober reflection we may conclude that our overeating and character defects were major contributing factors.

If we've cheated employers by inefficient performance due to binges, it may be too late to get the job back. But part of coming to terms with ourselves and our past may involve an apology.

Similarly, our divorce may be final. But we may want to acknowledge out loud to our former partner our responsibility in inflicting injury. (Never mind where the partner was wrong. These are our amends, not his or hers.)

There are no hard and fast rules. Each situation should be examined individually, preferably with the help of a trusted, objective third party. The purpose is not to wallow in abject self-accusation. We are simply expressing our genuine regret, either out loud or on paper, to those we have hurt.

Saying "I'm sorry" draws on the reserves of humility we have been building up through the steps. Apologizing will remove some of the defensive walls that have blocked us from love and understanding. Saying "I'm sorry" diffuses our victims' defenses and allows them to be generous. It can lead to the burial of past hostilities and to a fresh start. And the cost is only two words and a little pride.

What Do We Do After We Say We're Sorry?

Sometimes saying we're sorry is enough to heal hard feelings and to get a relationship back on the right track. However, making direct amends often requires something more—actions as well as words.

How many times have we said we're sorry for an episode of bad temper following a binge? After the first couple of hundred apologies, none of us is taken very seriously. Only by maintaining a positive change in our behavior for a substantial period of time will we convince those around us that we mean business.

We can start by explaining what we are learning about our illness and the program we are following to arrest it. We can ask our close friends and family members to help us. We can think of specific actions that will show the injured party that our remorse is genuine, and that we want to do our part to make the relationship better.

An obvious way of making amends is to stop overeating and start doing things for and with the person who has been hurt. With abstinence comes time, energy, and money that were not available when we were bingeing. How about using some of this new physical and emotional wealth for a weekly excursion with our children? A tennis or dancing class with our spouse? More frequent phone calls or visits to friends?

The most important thing we do after we say we're sorry is to change our behavior so that we stop harming those around us. If we have injured a coworker by malicious gossip, we can stop spreading rumors. We may never come to like the person, but we can strengthen our own program by apologizing and avoiding any further damaging remarks.

If we have stolen money or food, we will feel better if we replace it if possible. Perhaps we'll make a contribution to CARE or some other charity as a token means of restitution for having eaten more than our share of the world's food supply.

The behavior of a compulsive overeater during and after a binge can be remarkably similar to that of an alcoholic during and after a drunk. Thinking becomes irrational. We say things we don't mean. We can gravely damage anyone in our path. The best permanent amends to ourselves and everyone else will come through abstinence and working the program.

Members of Overeaters Anonymous who are living the program attest to the spiritual awakening that comes with abstinence. The OA program makes it possible to get off the emotional roller coaster we rode in the past and learn to function on a more even keel. Looking to a Higher Power for guidance frees us from self-centeredness, which made it difficult to get along with other people.

With God's help, we are becoming able to stop and think before lashing out in anger. We think about how the other person feels. We think about what our Higher Power wants us to do. We turn over a conflict situation to God before it gets out of control. This is Step Nine. This is making amends. Here and now we speak and act differently, avoiding the recurrence of past arguments and fights.

There are as many ways of making amends as there are injuries inflicted. The common threads that run through all of our efforts to make compensation for our mistakes are honesty, courage, and the sincere desire to know and do the will of our Higher Power.

Period of Reconstruction

In OA fellowship, we share our experience, strength, and hope. Every day, in meetings all over the United States and in foreign countries, moving personal stories of reconciliation are told. We discover that when we summon the courage to go directly to someone we have harmed and ask forgiveness, the bad feelings and hostility begin to disappear.

Then comes a time of rebuilding. This period of reconstruction is a continuing process. Just as we ask the God of our understanding for daily abstinence from compulsive overeating, we also ask for insight and strength to act according to God's will in all of our relationships. If family and friends have suffered from our defects, we now have tools to rebuild those relationships on a more solid foundation. Being honest about our shortcomings makes it possible for others to acknowledge their own. We are sharing our feelings rather than covering them up with food. Our new insight can help create an atmosphere of forgiveness and understanding on all sides.

If this doesn't happen immediately, don't be discouraged. Reconstruction takes time. There will be starts and stops, progress and delays. Perhaps other family members will be interested in learning more about the OA program, perhaps not. It will take time to convince them by word and deed that what we're doing is right for us. They may never understand. Sometimes family and friends will resent our investment of time and energy in OA meetings, our apparent inflexibility when it comes to what we eat and when we eat it, our phone calls to friends in the program.

When one member of a family changes, the others are affected. A compulsive overeater can be the victim of guilt and low self-esteem. He or she has often been willing to make all sorts of concessions to others in order to continue overeating. The compulsive overeater can easily have become the family doormat as well as the garbage can. When self-esteem is low, it is difficult to be assertive and stand up for legitimate rights.

All of this changes with abstinence. Self-respect returns and the doormat is no longer conveniently in place. The family status quo is upset, and adjustments need to be made.

Communication is vital. If we are not willing to let other people know where we are and what we are feeling, it is hard for them to be supportive and understanding. In the process of making amends and cleaning house with family and friends, we not only apologize to them for our past mistakes but also tell them what we are trying to do right now, in the present.

It's possible that our efforts will be met with disbelief, suspicion, or out-and-out hostility. Other people may feel threatened if we are not very careful to focus only on our own defects and mistakes. Or the family may come to the conclusion that this time we're really into something weird. Perhaps what we most fear is that we'll be laughed at or that someone else will take advantage of our vulnerability.

Let's remember that what we're trying to do is put the past out of the way so that we can free ourselves to live in the present. We are taking the necessary steps toward our personal recovery from compulsive overeating. The more comfortable our relationships with the important others in our lives, the less likely we will be to expect food to fulfill needs it cannot fulfill.

Along with love goes the power to hurt deeply. Disturbed family relationships put our abstinence in danger. If a family situation is intolerable, we may have to extract ourselves eventually in the interest of self-preservation. But first, with the help of a Higher Power, we need to do everything possible to make amends for our part in the conflict. As we get ourselves straightened out, we just may find that the conflict begins to abate.

Being patient and turning our lives over to the God of our understanding on a daily basis make it possible to rebuild relationships that may have seemed hopelessly deteriorated. Since a Higher Power is in charge and the results of our amends are in the hands of that Higher Power, we do not need to fear the outcome. All we have to do is proceed one day at a time according to the inner guidance we receive. We may not be sure exactly where we are headed, but as long as we stay in touch with the God of our understanding and work the program, we will travel in the right direction.

Grace

In the same way that abstinence requires the grace of a Higher Power, so does reconciliation. Grace turns a stammered, embarrassed apology into a building block with which two people can begin to reconstruct a marriage. Grace heals the wounds of misunderstanding between a parent and a teenager and at least partially bridges the generation gap. Grace is what makes our less-than-perfect efforts sufficient for the situation, whatever it is.

If we have no way of knowing how to contact a person we've harmed, or if the person is no longer living, we nevertheless can be emotionally willing to make amends if it were possible. We can pray that any lingering resentment on our part be removed, and we can wholeheartedly forgive the other person. Although "there may be some wrongs we can never fully right, we don't worry about them if we can honestly say to ourselves that we would right them if we could" (Big Book, p. 83).

The Promises

It's probably not by chance that the promises of the program, which are given in the Big Book of Alcoholics Anonymous, come directly after the discussion of Step Nine. When we get beyond merely thinking about making amends and actually go out and *make* them, we reap an astonishing harvest of benefits.

If we are painstaking about this phase of our development, we will be amazed before we are halfway through. We are going to know a new freedom and a new happiness. We will not regret the past nor wish to shut the door on it. We will comprehend the word serenity and we will know peace. No matter how far down the scale we have gone, we will see how our experience can benefit others. Those feelings of uselessness and self-pity will disappear. We will lose interest in selfish things and gain interest in our fellows. Self-seeking will slip away. Our whole attitude and outlook on life will change. Fear of people and of economic insecurity will leave us. We will intuitively know how to handle situations which used to baffle us. We will suddenly realize that God is doing for us what we could not do for ourselves.

Are these extravagant promises? We think not. They are being fulfilled among us — sometimes quickly, sometimes slowly. They will always materialize if we work for them. (Big Book, pp. 83–84)

If what the program promises seems too good to be true, how about doing some careful research before dismissing the possibility that the good things could actually happen? Go to enough meetings to hear and see how these promises are being fulfilled among ordinary people who are seriously working the program. Do the footwork. Make phone calls. Read the literature. Check with sponsors. Turn your will, life, abstinence problems—everything—over to the care of God as you understand him. Pray only for the knowledge of God's will and the power to carry that out.

Again and again it has been proved that the program works if we work it. Worthwhile results require effort and action; they do not happen by themselves. This program is no exception.

The details of how the promises are fulfilled will vary according to the individual circumstances. One person finally becomes able to go out and get a job after being isolated at home with cookies and television. Another can walk into a room full of strangers without wanting to run and hide. Someone else finds that a paralyzing fear of being on an airplane can be controlled.

Close friends are made, where formerly we had none. Compulsive spending disappears and with it the terrifying pile of bills. Where before we worried obsessively about any threatening situation, we become able to handle what each day brings as it comes along. We discover our intuitive knowledge. We "suddenly realize that God is doing for us what we could not do for ourselves."

How are the OA promises related to making amends? Guilt and resentments shut us off from the freedom and peace of our Higher Power. We need to clear our lives of this emotional debris.

It is difficult, if not impossible, to be on good terms with a Higher Power if we are harboring ill will toward our fellow human beings. After making amends to the best of our ability, we no longer have hard feelings standing between us and the grace of the God of our understanding. Step Nine is not easy. Neither are the other steps and neither is life. But the rewards are great.

Step Ten

ACCEPTING OURSELVES

Continued to take personal inventory and when we were wrong promptly admitted it.

Now that you have arrived at the tenth Step in the Overeaters Anonymous program, you are ready to maintain your recovery one day at a time for as long as you live. We use the last three Steps to stay in touch with ourselves, our Higher Power, and others in a positive, creative way. The maintenance Steps define a new way of life, one that increasingly becomes a spiritual adventure and a physically and emotionally fulfilling experience.

As compulsive overeaters, we finally realize that the "more" that satisfies us without harm comes by way of spiritual growth. We have made progress through the first nine Steps — progress in turning our lives over to the God of our understanding, in getting rid of the mental and emotional liabilities that prevent us from knowing and doing God's will, and in cultivating assets such as courage, humility, and understanding. This is spiritual growth. Its possibilities are infinite, and each day brings new challenges and opportunities. There will always be more to learn. We are rewarded with inner satisfactions that fill the emptiness we formerly tried to fill with excess food.

The way to keep our program alive and well, and thus to maintain abstinence from compulsive overeating, is to continue growing. In this life there is no standing still; we are either moving forward or backsliding. The same holds true for our illness. We are either getting better or getting worse; we do not stay the same. Recovery implies continuing effort on our part, but of course we are not working alone. The daily reprieve that we are granted comes from a Higher Power and depends on our spiritual condition, as well as on the footwork we do. Step Ten helps us to stay attuned to ourselves, our Higher Power, and other people during the ongoing process of recovery.

Sooner or later, most of us are convinced that the practice of abstinence affects our emotional and spiritual lives as well as what we eat. Negative emotions, such as anger and self-pity, destroy serenity and can trigger binges. A negative spiritual state—for instance, giving way to pride, greed, doubt, or dishonesty—is equally damaging. If we lose touch with our Higher Power and let our emotions run riot, we will probably do all sorts of harm to ourselves and those around us, and we will be in danger of slipping back into compulsive overeating. To avoid backsliding, we need to keep building up assets like honesty, courage, faith, responsibility, understanding, and love for others.

Maintaining our program is literally a life-and-death choice. OA offers a way of controlling a progressive illness, which if not treated can destroy its victims. The Twelve Steps have proved successful in arresting the illness. It has also been proved that one can stop practicing the Steps, drop out of the program, and commit slow suicide (sometimes not so slow).

Experience indicates that once we become compulsive overeaters, our potential for abusing food is always present. It is very easy to fall back into old habits. We are offered a new life of recovery, but this gift depends on daily attention to our emotional and spiritual development. No one else is going to do it for us. If we want the benefits promised by the program, we have to do our part. There is no graduation ceremony, but there is gratifying progress as we go to meetings, work the Steps, and stay in touch with a Higher Power.

What's Going On

Step Ten suggests that we continue taking personal inventory and promptly admit our mistakes. This Step is a tool that helps us to be honest about what's really happening in our lives and to make immediate amends when we see that we are wrong. Step Ten is crucial to the continued improvement of interpersonal relationships, which in turn makes it easier to abstain from compulsive overeating. We maintain our willingness to admit where we are at fault in a conflict, and we are also willing to forgive when someone else has made a mistake. We do not have to fall back on the unsatisfactory consolation of excessive eating.

How do you know when to take an inventory? Many of us find it helpful to practice the tenth Step at the end of each day—to go over our actions and attitudes during that particular twenty-four-hour period. Was our abstinence cleaner? Did we refrain from criticizing the people we live with? Did we make a useful contribution to someone else's day? In this daily self-examination we review where we made progress with the program and where we got off the track, considering how to repair any damage we may have done and how to avoid the same mistakes tomorrow. We congratulate ourselves for positive actions and feelings (as well as for temptations overcome), and we reaffirm our relationship with a Higher Power.

At any hour of the day, if we are getting upset or feeling that our abstinence is threatened, it is time to stop and take a quick inventory. In the *Twelve Steps and Twelve Traditions*, this part of Step Ten is called a spot check. If we are angry with a coworker and feel our serenity slipping, we don't have to wait until we hit the ceiling or our colleague before we stop to think. We are not responsible for what someone else does, but we are responsible for our reactions. We have a choice as to how we will act in a given situation. If we're upset, that's our problem, and we need to deal with it. For instance, if we see that our anger is coming out of false pride, we can choose to let go of it. A spot-check inventory reveals how our attitude toward and response to events beyond our control, such as someone else's words or actions, can strengthen rather than weaken our recovery.

There are also circumstances that call for a major housecleaning at least once a year. Have new problems accumulated since we took our fourth Step? Are the same old problems coming back? If for a period of time we have been feeling confused and out of touch with ourselves, those around us, or our Higher Power, we may need to actually sit down and write out another inventory for review with our sponsor or someone else. We might plan for an annual review, similar to a yearly physical examination, as a preventive measure.

However we decide to use Step Ten, we have a program that offers a plan of action when something is wrong. This is one of the reasons we can be grateful that we are recovering compulsive overeaters. We have a built-in compass that tells us when we're off course. When we begin to have trouble with food, emotions, other people, or all of them together, we can be sure that we have wandered away from the program and from our Higher Power. We can be grateful that by way of the illness we have found a new guide for living. Because of our weakness, we have turned to a Power greater than ourselves, a source of strength that we otherwise might not have experienced.

Do you find yourself waking up in the clutches of some dreadful anxiety that sets your mind going in circles? Do you go through too many days with a cloud of self-pity hanging over your head? Are you caught in a relationship that you know is harmful?

Our tendency is to blame circumstances and other people for whatever is wrong in our lives. As the program keeps reminding us, this is counterproductive. We are powerless over other people and events. What we can do is take our inventory, see where our own liabilities are getting in the way of our program, and admit our part in whatever conflict is destroying our serenity.

This may happen many times a day. How often do you try to control the people around you, dictating their actions and then getting mad when they do not do what you think they should? The sooner you realize what you are doing, apologize, and back off, the sooner your energy will be free for constructive action. Rather than allowing a conflict to grow, we can do something about it immediately if we recognize our part in it and turn the angry feelings over to a Higher Power. Stop and think before you say or do something you will later regret. Let go of self-will. Let the other person be right. Let your Higher Power determine the outcome of events, even such simple ones as what will happen if your friend doesn't listen to your directions and gets lost.

As compulsive overeaters, we have all used food to mask our feelings. "Oh no, nothing is wrong," you said to yourself and everyone else, in spite of the fact that you were filled with resentment because someone let you down. And then you ate. None of us has to do that anymore. We have a program, and we have tools. We can admit, especially to ourselves, that there is a problem, and we can proceed to find out what it is and what can be done about it. (Did you feel let down because your expectations were unrealistic?) Remember, in any given situation we are only responsible for taking our own personal inventory.

Name Them, Claim Them, Dump Them

The advantage of taking inventory when we are awash with negative emotions is that we are able to recognize the feelings, admit that we own and are responsible for them, and then let them go. We do not have to hang on to painful emotions or use them as an excuse to overeat; we can choose to turn them over—again and again. "Let go and let God."

Writing is one of the valuable tools of the OA program. When you are not sure just what it is that is troubling you, take out paper and pencil and put down in black and white what you are feeling. Instead of going into a "blue funk," snapping at your best friend, and heading for the nearest fast-food restaurant, write! Write until your pencil begins to reveal what is really going on inside your head.

This stream-of-consciousness inventory can be for our eyes only. If we know before we start what is bothering us, writing can be a way of getting rid of it. The very act of putting our feelings into words on paper helps to dissipate the anger, fear, resentment, or self-pity. When we look at what we have written, we may see our previously overwhelming emotional reaction shrink to manageable size. Then we can tear up the paper instead of hurling invectives at the person we live with or stuffing ourselves with food.

Sometimes we may want to go over what we have written with another person. Should I look for a new job? Ask for a raise? From fifth Step experience, we know that sharing our hurts, fears, guilts, and anxieties liberates us from them. In the past we attempted to be independent and manage our own lives and our own problems, but that didn't work. We have now learned enough humility through these Steps that we can go to a trusted friend or sponsor for help when we need it. Often the other person can assist simply by being a sounding board. Defining a problem out loud to another makes it more manageable; chasing it around and around the same old solitary mental track only makes things worse. Someone else can often hear what we are saying behind and underneath our actual words, and their perception puts the situation into a new light.

Regularly looking inward to identify the reason we're upset works wonders with relationships. If we see that our desire to be in control has triggered a fight with our spouse, we can admit it, say we're sorry, and let go. When the insight occurs sooner rather than later, much emotional pain can be avoided. Though we can probably *name* our partner's character defects more easily than our own, ours are the only ones we are able to claim and dump.

Step Ten gives us a way to take our emotional and spiritual temperature and apply treatment when needed. Once we identify and admit where we have been wrong, we can choose to let go of those mistakes and any regrets attached to them. If we are in contact with a Higher Power, we are living *now*, not in the past. We cannot change what has happened. To regret what we cannot change is to keep ourselves bound to the past instead of alive to God's will for our lives here and now. Self-examination helps us to learn from past mistakes, but we do not need to dwell on them. We were wrong; we see that now. We have said that we are sorry. Since we believe that our Higher Power forgives us, we can forgive ourselves and move on, preferably out of the kitchen.

Forgiveness—of others and ourselves, repeated over and over—is a prerequisite to letting go of negative feelings. We do not need to wallow in guilt over mistakes. It has been pointed out that excess guilt can be an inverse form of pride; we expect ourselves to be perfect. By promptly admitting where we were wrong, we can avoid self-imposed guilt trips. We will never be perfect, but we are learning and making progress.

New Possibilities

We can try to stop making unreasonable demands upon those we love. We can show kindness where we had shown none. With those we dislike we can begin to practice justice and courtesy, perhaps going out of our way to understand and help them. (Twelve and Twelve, p. 93)

Gradually, we are moving off center stage. When we discover that clinging to self-will defeats us every time, we can abandon our attempts to satisfy the great "I want." Just as abstinence teaches us to eat what we need, so the Steps of the OA program teach the art of give and take. As we become more committed to knowing and doing God's will, it grows easier to think about the needs and feelings of other people. Honestly trying to do what a Higher Power wants us to do, we can be more tolerant, more fair, and more generous, even with individuals we don't particularly like. The reward is that we end up feeling better ourselves.

Through this program, we are learning how to live comfortably without escaping into excess food. For a time, this may make us more vulnerable to emotional ups and downs. Along with being dependent on food to cushion the hard knocks of living, we may also have been overly dependent on other people, expecting them to cater to our whims. Gradually, we are relinquishing our frustrating attempts to control and manipulate.

Although moving off center stage means that we are considerably easier to live with, we are certainly not going to turn into saints. The difference is that now we are better able to catch ourselves when we are winding up for conflict and more willing to say, "Excuse me. I didn't mean to step on you. I don't expect you to read my mind and to satisfy my every wish. Let's just agree to be human together. When something hurts, we can say 'ouch' without starting the Third World War."

When we don't take ourselves too seriously, and when we don't always have to be right and in control, conflicts abate. In Step Three, when we turned our wills and our lives over to the God of our understanding, we agreed that God would run the show, and we are trying to act according to his direction. This means being willing to let go of whatever separates us from our Higher Power—fear, anger, pride, resentment—because as recovering compulsive overeaters we cannot afford these negative feelings, no matter how convinced we are that they are justified. We know from sad experience that negative emotions, justified or not, will undermine our recovery.

With spiritual growth comes greater tolerance of the weaknesses of other people. Now that we know we are being cared for by a Higher Power, we do not have to hang on to impossibly high expectations of our fellow human beings. They are struggling, too, and like us are doing the best they can. Our security and self-esteem no longer depend on the illusion of having perfect friends, an ideal partner, exemplary children, or all-wise parents.

When we were overeating, most of us did not like ourselves or anyone else. Through abstinence and the Twelve Steps, we discover, often slowly, that the source of friction between ourselves and others is within us. When we are in harmony internally, it is possible to be in harmony with those around us as well. It is possible to let go of unreasonable demands. When we can accept and begin to like ourselves, we can be more generous with everyone else. We discover that being part of the chorus can be a lot more enjoyable than fighting to stay on center stage.

Tenth-Stepping with Love

This is a good place to remember that inventory-taking is not always done in red ink. It's a poor day indeed when we haven't done *something* right. As a matter of fact, the waking hours are usually well-filled with things that are constructive. Good intentions, good thoughts, and good acts are there for us to see. Even when we have tried hard and failed, we may chalk that up as one of the greatest credits of all. (Twelve and Twelve, p. 93)

What have we done right today? Did we take a few moments to talk to someone who seemed to need cheering up? Did we put the top back on the toothpaste tube without criticizing the person who left it off? Did we try again to have an abstinent day?

Important as it is, abstinence alone does not fill our lives. Abstinence frees us from compulsive overeating so that we can love ourselves and other people and turn our energies toward productive, enjoyable activities. If we are abstaining out of a sense of "ought," or in order to be "good," or so that we can wear a size eight, we will probably run out of steam before very long.

Tenth-stepping with love means that we forgive ourselves when certain actions do not measure up to the standards we have set. We come home tired and uptight over a problem at the office. We make mincemeat out of nine-year-old Billy, who has left his bicycle in the middle of the driveway for the eighty-seventh time, eat four doughnuts, and kick the dog. Not so good.

When the dust settles, and we are back on the track, after having telephoned a friend in the program, read some OA literature, or simply spent several minutes quietly getting in touch with our Higher Power, the first thing we do is make peace with Billy. Then we forgive ourselves for breaking our abstinence and being a "rotten parent." (And we pet the dog.) Then we think about how we can avoid some of the stress and fatigue that sabotage our recovery. Perhaps we even glimpse how a change in our attitude could improve things at the office.

Tenth-stepping with love means that we refrain from playing games with other people's feelings. If we have landed in a relationship in which we are using another person in a selfish, dependent way, but are unwilling to make a genuine commitment, Step Ten says we need to admit that to ourselves and to the other person. Honesty may not be easy, but not being honest is harder in the long run. Besides, when we are being straight with ourselves and others, we do not need to overeat.

Tenth-stepping with love means that we look for ways to fill our lives with positive experiences. As we take inventory in the OA program, we measure our wealth not by what we have in stock but by what we have given away. We look for opportunities to be of service to other people. We are willing to try and to fail and to try again. We care. We are alive. We are learning—one day at a time.

Step Eleven

CENTERING OURSELVES

Sought through prayers and meditation to improve our conscious contact with God *as we understood Him*, praying only for knowledge of His will for us and the power to carry that out.

Step Eleven spells out what we have been trying to do all along, perhaps even before we found the Overeaters Anonymous program. The presence of a Higher Power is a reality deep within each one of us, attracting our consciousness like a magnetic field. In the eleventh Step, we reaffirm our desire and decision to know and do the will of this Higher Power. Through prayer and meditation, we want to improve our conscious contact with the God of our understanding.

How we take this Step is a choice we make according to individual preference. There are many ways to pray and meditate, and each of us is free to have a personal understanding of a Higher Power. The program is big and broad enough to accommodate all of us, for the only requirement of OA membership is the desire to stop overeating.

What makes the Twelve Step programs uniquely effective is that they offer a guide to spiritual growth. When we find that we cannot stop overeating compulsively without coming to know and rely on a Power greater than ourselves, we see how Step Eleven is central to our plan of recovery. Though practice of the Step may be sporadic at first, we will keep returning to it because it works. Many of us are convinced that our periods of prayer and meditation have become the best time of the day, and that regular use of the eleventh Step is the heart of our recovery program. In these quiet moments, we recharge our batteries by getting in touch with the source of our strength, and we find direction for our lives one day at a time. Prayer and meditation keep us alive and growing.

Centering

If prayer and meditation are new to you, consider that you are embarking on an inner voyage of exploration and discovery. If "the only scoffers at prayer are those who never tried it enough" (Twelve and Twelve, p. 97), then making a commitment to practice Step Eleven on a daily basis will be a way of demonstrating its effectiveness in your life. When we are willing to try to improve our conscious contact with a Higher Power, we are open to whatever insight comes our way. The longer we work the OA program, the more we become convinced that each day we are given exactly what we need.

Beginning the morning with a few quiet minutes gives us composure and links us with a source of strength and peace beyond ourselves. One way to start is with the Serenity Prayer: "God, grant me the serenity to accept the things I cannot change, the courage to change the things I can, and the wisdom to know the difference."

Many of us use one or more of the daily meditation books that have been published for members of Twelve Step programs. After reading the thought for the day, which may include a short prayer, some of us like to let our minds be quiet and take time to listen for an inner voice.

It has been suggested that praying is asking a question and that meditating is listening for the answer. At the beginning, we may spend most of our time telling our Higher Power what is going on and where we are. Gradually, we learn to center ourselves and be receptive to the thoughts and feelings that rise gently from down deep instead of chasing those that are spinning around the top of our head. This has been described as thinking God's thoughts after him.

With practice, prayer and meditation become tools for an ongoing relationship that recreates us each time we make contact. We know that we are in touch with the spiritual base of our lives, and we don't have to do, say, or think anything. We can just *be*.

As compulsive overeaters, many of us pray first of all for abstinence: *If it is your will, God, give me abstinence just for today. I cannot do it alone*. We can come back to this prayer as often as necessary. It reminds us that we have turned over our wills and our lives along with our abstinence. Each time we remember, we are touching and centering ourselves in a Higher Power.

Meditation for Serenity

What, for some of us, used to be periods of anxiety and terror can become times of creative meditation and spiritual growth. Although abstinence from compulsive overeating is our goal, this does not automatically guarantee tranquillity. It often happens that the fears we have tried to suppress with excess food will push to the surface of our awareness when we stop using food as a tranquilizer. If we are not going to eat over this fear, what are we going to do? What do you do when you wake up in the middle of the night gripped by a nameless anxiety or convinced of some impending disaster?

If we believe that a Higher Power has put us where we are for a reason and that we are in exactly the place we should be, then we can partially detach ourselves from the emotional storm raging inside and wait quietly for it to pass. In the process we will undoubtedly learn something we did not know before, or something we knew but would not face. The fears we try to avoid and deny are the ones that develop into panic. Let your fear surface. Give it a name. Be willing to feel it. Then ask yourself if the God of your understanding wants you to be afraid.

Since your Higher Power is in charge of your life, you are not alone with whatever it is you face. Moment by moment, you will be given the strength you need. We lose jobs and loved ones. We live with frustration and illness. Chaos may appear to swirl around us, but if our inner perception is grounded in God's reality, here and now, we will not be swept away by fear or try to escape through overeating.

With daily practice, the quiet time of meditation extends order to the busy hours and begins to erase irrational fears. As we go deeper into the stillness within, we find ourselves in a place where there is increasing love and decreasing fear. If we go *through* our fear, not trying to cover it up or escape, we will come out on the other side realizing that the fear was not a solid wall after all.

The key that unlocks the treasure of Step Eleven is regular use. We set aside a definite period of time every day when we will be available to our Higher Power, and we follow whatever individual plan we have for prayer and meditation, whether or not we feel like it. Call it spiritual exercise, if you wish. Serenity is a spiritual muscle developed with training and concentration. It does not fall into our laps out of the blue. If we want the inner peace and serenity that come from conscious contact with the God of our understanding, we have to be willing to take the time to cultivate the relationship. Remembering the program slogan, "keep it simple," we may have to postpone or eliminate some of our other activities if they get in the way.

First Things First

Setting priorities is essential if we are to work the Steps of the program and maintain abstinence from compulsive overeating. Since millions of ideas, impulses, requests, desires, and demands compete every day for our attention and energy, there is no way we can or should act on more than a tiny fraction of them. If we go off in all directions, the resulting fatigue and chaos not only destroy serenity but also threaten abstinence.

The minutes we spend quietly getting in touch with ourselves and our Higher Power will multiply our effectiveness in everything we do throughout the day. When we are focused and integrated, we get to the heart of whatever needs to be done without wasting unnecessary time and effort. How often did you spin your wheels when you were overeating? The disorder and frustration of those days can be put behind you now that you have a program for living and a way to sort out what is important.

If you wake up in the morning not knowing where to start or how you can possibly do all the things you think ought to be done, ask for help. Ask your Higher Power to direct your thoughts and your actions, setting your priorities for the next twenty-four hours. Ask again and again during the day, whenever you feel confused. Remember that the answer is not likely to be found in the refrigerator.

As we go through the Steps to recovery, we examine our lives and find that in many cases what used to be important and time-consuming is no longer of much value. Trying to impress others, grasping all we can get, winning arguments and being right, hanging on to the past, trying to rearrange the world to suit us—this compulsive behavior is tiring and self-defeating. When we are in contact with a Reality beyond our own egos, we can live each moment according to inner direction and "go with the flow" instead of trying to swim upstream. Our priorities are sorted out according to what seems right in relation to a Higher Power.

Letting God determine what is important may appear to be a shaky and frightening procedure at first. What if it doesn't work? But then, how well did we do when we were following the dictates of self-will? Being open and willing to try what has worked for other people in the program has brought us this far and will take us through Step Eleven. We may not be able to explain how prayer and meditation work, but when we experience firsthand the positive difference they make in our lives, we will have a growing faith in their effectiveness.

Learning what we need to do in order to maintain abstinence and stay on track emotionally and spiritually is a process of self-discovery that proceeds by trial and error. We are not likely to be struck by thunderbolts of revelation during our periods of meditation. What we do encounter is a slowly growing sense of assurance and relatedness, faith that we are being cared for and directed. Returning to this inner place several times each day becomes our number one priority, the starting point from which everything else falls into place.

To Know God's Will

When we get tangled up in conflicting shoulds, oughts, and wants, it helps to remember that Step Eleven suggests we pray "only for knowledge of God's will for us and the power to carry that out" (Twelve and Twelve, p. 102). This simple recommendation cuts a straight path through a maze of anxiety and indecision. It is a direct route to serenity.

If we decide ahead of time what we want for ourselves or someone else or the state of the union, and if we pray for that to happen, we will probably be disappointed and disillusioned if events turn out otherwise. If we had all the answers, we would not need a Higher Power. The fact of the matter is, we often do not know what is best for ourselves, other people, or the world in general, and even if we did, we do not have the ability to manipulate external events. Trying to run even our own small corner of the world is a wearisome and defeating experience.

How much more rewarding it is to pray that God's will be done, since that puts us on the side of reality! Thinking in terms of God's will rather than self-will means that we can relax our efforts to figure everything out. If we pray sincerely to know what our Higher Power wants us to do in a given situation, we can assume that the answer will come without a lot of worry and indecision. It may not come today, but when we need to act, we can trust that we will be guided. In the meantime, a good rule of thumb is *when in doubt, don't.* When action is necessary, we do the best we can according to the insight we possess at the time, and if we make a mistake we can try again.

How do we know God's will for our lives? How can we be sure that we are not rationalizing our own desires into the will of a Higher Power? Here is where the support of other people in the program becomes an important part of Step Eleven. We do not have to make far-reaching decisions by ourselves. Someone we trust can be a sounding board when we are not sure which course of action to take. Believing that a Higher Power works through other people also, we can expect to have many of our questions answered through dialogue with those who are our companions in this spiritual journey.

Another test is that of time. If we are headed in the wrong direction, we're going to realize it sooner or later. The longer and more conscientiously we work the Steps, the earlier we are able to recognize and correct a faulty course of action.

Experience indicates that we get into trouble when we try to see too far ahead. We do not need to know God's will for us for next week or next year or the rest of our lives. Since this is a one-day-at-a-time program, we are only concerned with knowing and doing the will of a Higher Power now, today. We can pray that our thoughts and actions today will be on target and leave the future in God's hands.

We can also leave in God's hands his will for other people. We are "praying only for knowledge of His will for us." The decision of what is best for someone else is not ours to make, difficult as it may be to let go. Even when we are convinced that we know what someone close to us should or should not do, the program teaches us to detach with love. We respect each individual's right to live his or her own life. Though we may do all we can to help those we care about, the ultimate responsibility rests between them and the God of their understanding.

Power to Do It

Most of us have more than a glimmer of an idea of what God's will for us might include. The crunch comes when we think about actually carrying out some of these possibilities. Often, we find ourselves in a position where "the spirit is willing but the flesh is weak."

As an example, we may assume that our Higher Power's will for us is abstinence from compulsive overeating and from emotional and spiritual destruction. In Step Eleven we pray for the strength to do our part in maintaining this abstinence. It is not enough to know what is good for us; we need to do the footwork that brings about the desired results. We can pray and meditate by ourselves, but this does not mean that we no longer need the support of the group to maintain our program of recovery.

Whatever we focus on for the day, we will be sustained in our efforts by the fact that others are working along similar lines. After you have asked for the strength to be abstinent, make a phone call to reinforce your intent. Get to a meeting if you feel yourself slipping into an emotional binge. There is strength in the fellowship, which carries over into the times when we are alone and unsure.

Often, the courage to take the first faltering step on a course of action will generate the power to take another step, and another, and another. The miracle of this program is the positive change it effects in our lives. When we are willing to move ahead, however tentatively, growth is possible. We make the first move toward a new job, a new relationship, a new commitment, not knowing exactly what the outcome will be but with the faith that we will have guidance and strength to continue, if it is God's will.

The eleventh Step points our way toward becoming a channel for the action of a Higher Power. Time spent improving our conscious contact means that we will have something to pass on to the people with whom we interact. Increasingly, we come to believe that the challenges and blessings of each day are ours for a reason. Other people cross our paths because we have something to give them and receive from them. Don't forget, we are no longer trying to run the show. Since we are sincerely seeking to know God's will, we can ask for the insight to give and receive at a deeply meaningful level.

We came into Overeaters Anonymous admitting that we were powerless over food and unable to manage our own lives. We declared physical, emotional, and spiritual bankruptcy. Gradually, we are building a new life based on a Power beyond ourselves. Insights come, and along with them comes the strength to act on these insights. Our willingness to act and the actions themselves give rise to new insights. We learn, and we become stronger, whether our efforts are directed toward following a food plan or determining what other things we need to do in order to like ourselves and live with those around us. Power to do God's will is available to us. Our job is to ask for it—often—and use it.

Wearing the World as a Loose Garment

We have found that the actual good results of prayer are beyond question. They are matters of knowledge and experience. All those who have persisted have found strength not ordinarily their own. They have found wisdom beyond their usual capability. And they have increasingly found a peace of mind which can stand firm in the face of difficult circumstances. (Twelve and Twelve, p. 104)

Difficult circumstances have a way of cropping up persistently. None of us is exempt. What we are offered in this program, especially through Step Eleven, is a way of life that keeps us from being overwhelmed and from turning to excess food as a crutch. Friends die and bills pile up. Accidents, injuries, and conflicts are an inevitable part of being alive. Through prayer and meditation we can find a center of calm beneath the daily turbulence. We will still feel grief, pain, anxiety, and anger, but these emotions will not blind or destroy us. Conscious contact with the God of our understanding gives us a core of serenity that no amount of trouble can shatter.

Our serenity may be temporarily submerged by pressing concerns, but we know it still exists in that quiet place within and that all we have to do is take time to go back there. Storms will come, but they will pass. Experience shows us that the sooner we turn the problems over to a Higher Power, the sooner we get back to serenity. The less we allow ourselves to be caught up in the pursuit of possessions, prestige, material security, and ego satisfaction, the more inner peace we will have. This is wearing the world as a loose garment.

Material satisfactions by themselves are not enough. We need daily spiritual nourishment in order to stay strong and healthy. When we give priority to getting ourselves together spiritually, the rest of the world slides into place—loosely and without pressure. We cope with the problems and logistics of our existence without getting bogged down in secondary considerations and without overeating. If we are "praying only for the knowledge of [God's] will for our lives and the power to carry that out" (Big Book, p. 59), we will not fall apart if someone we love leaves us or if we lose a job. We will hurt; we will be afraid; but we will not be destroyed.

Improving our conscious contact with a Higher Power makes life an adventure instead of a chore. We get in touch with the source of our own creativity. We see new options. We gain the courage to take risks and exercise these creative options. We will have failures and we will have successes, but whatever the results, we are grounded in a source of strength beyond ourselves.

LIVING THE PROGRAM

Having had a spiritual awakening as the result of these steps, we tried to carry this message to compulsive overeaters and to practice these principles in all our affairs.

A new member of Overeaters Anonymous remarked at a meeting that the last ten years were little more than a blur in her memory. Since compulsive overeating had taken over her life (round-the-clock food consumption was the rule rather than the exception), she was hardly aware of what she had done other than eat during those years.

Not all of us have suffered so severely from food abuse, but we all know what happens when eating gets out of control, and we see where we are headed if left to our own devices.

Fortunately, there is an answer, a means of arresting the destructive habit of compulsive overeating. The Twelve Steps, which have led so many to recovery from gambling, drinking, drug using, and other kinds of addictive behavior, offer a new life to those of us who are powerless over food.

Because we were desperate, because we could not find a way out of our problems alone, and because we saw miracles of recovery occurring in the lives of others, we decided to reach for help from a Power greater than ourselves. Gradually, we began to be aware of this Higher Power in the OA group, in the events of every day, and deep in the quiet of our own hearts. The Steps of the program have taken us through surrender, self-examination, willingness to let go of our own character defects, and the sincere attempt to make amends in order to improve our relationships. Each Step brings us into closer contact with the God of our understanding, and we begin to wake up physically, emotionally, and spiritually.

Abstinence from the kind and quantity of food that was slowly but surely destroying us means that we can feel good physically. After an abstinent day, we can wake up the next morning alert and alive, with an inner joy. We start experiencing emotions again that had been suppressed by excess calories.

Our bodies and emotions have new life and so do our spirits. The longer we are in this program, the more firmly we believe that the spiritual awakening is what triggers all of the improvements. There simply is no other explanation. Sometimes the awakening happens suddenly; more often it is a gradual process.

"Having had a spiritual awakening as a result of these steps . . ." That says a lot. We may spend the rest of our lives discovering just how much. Waking up to our real selves and becoming aware of our relationship with a Higher Power is a gift. Our part is to become ready to receive the gift, and in order to be ready we work the Steps.

A spiritual awakening does not occur on demand, but there are things we can do in preparation. We can contact other people who demonstrate a spiritual strength in their lives. We can have an open mind and suspend our disbelief if we tend to be cynical about whatever our intellects alone cannot probe. If we have been preoccupied with material needs and desires, we can wake up to the fact that we may have been missing something!

A spiritual awakening may come when we are bored and feel suffocated by our unsuccessful attempts to satisfy our physical cravings. We can see that we have reached a dead end, and if we are receptive to trying an alternative route, other travelers can show us a new way that will take us where we want to go, thus becoming our spiritual guides.

Waking up is full of surprises. We realize that many of our old ideas have become excess baggage, and we decide to get rid of them. We find that we are better off without some of the people we thought we needed. We discover that we are tuned in to individuals we formerly did not understand. Because we are linked to a new source of strength, we can lay old fears to rest and pick up new options, risks, and responsibilities. When we accept the challenge that the life of the spirit offers, we find answers to boredom and emptiness. Days that used to pass in a blur of overeating are sharply defined by new activity and experiences. The spiritual awakening attested to in Step Twelve is a quiet internal revolution that gently propels us into a new state of consciousness. We become new people.

Sharing the Wealth

Perhaps the most important message of our program is that we cannot keep it unless we give it away. "Practical experience shows that nothing will so much insure immunity from [compulsive overeating] as intensive work with other [compulsive overeaters]" (Big Book, p. 89).

Carrying the message to other compulsive overeaters and sharing the new life we find in OA are ways of giving service and at the same time of continuing our own growth and recovery. When we work with a newcomer, we hear and see ourselves as we used to be. We are reminded of who we are and where we came from. When we tell someone else about the program, we reinforce our own conviction of its importance in our lives. Active participation in meetings and frequent telephone conversations with other members keep strength and support circulating among us. When we are working the Steps, we are walking examples of the program in action. The example we present says more than any number of words.

> Life will take on new meaning. To watch people recover, to see them help others, to watch loneliness vanish, to see a fellowship grow up about you, to have a host of friends – this is an experience you must not miss. . . . Frequent contact with newcomers and with each other is the bright spot of our lives. (Big Book, p. 89)

We can share our program with other interested people by providing literature and listings of area meetings, and by offering to take them with us when we go to meetings.

Basically, ours is a program of attraction rather than promotion, and it is not for everyone. If your enthusiasm for OA is met with skepticism, you can assume that the other person is not ready to hear about the program. At the very least, you will have planted a seed, and who knows when it may bear fruit? You will have done your part in carrying the message, whether or not it is favorably received.

It is true that those of us who have experienced that pain of compulsive overeating feel a tremendous amount of empathy for those who still suffer from the illness. We've been there; we know what it's like. We can offer our understanding, insight, and support, but we cannot force the program on anyone else, regardless of how much we think that person needs it.

It is well to be aware at the outset that some of our twelfth Step work will seem futile and frustrating. Along with the effects of all our other efforts, we turn the results of this step over to a Higher Power. The input is our responsibility; the outcome is not.

Sometimes we may be reluctant to talk about OA with people who are not familiar with the program. Are we embarrassed about labeling ourselves as compulsive overeaters? Are we hesitant to talk about a Higher Power and the spiritual aspects of the program?

How were you introduced to OA? Did you embrace the program immediately, or was there a period of time required before you were convinced that OA could help you? How grateful are you for hearing about it? It is the joy and gratitude we feel for at last having a solution to our number one problem that is contagious and that prompts us to spread the good news.

Often, the people our Higher Power puts in our path are those with whom we share our program. If we are alert to receive the signals that come to us every day, there will undoubtedly be many opportunities to help others and thus sustain our own recovery. We can put ourselves in situations that guarantee such opportunities—meetings, for example. Do you make an effort to talk to newcomers? To exchange phone numbers? To share on an increasingly deep and meaningful level with your program friends?

Each of us has a unique story to tell. As we come out of our isolation, we can pass on the benefits of our individual experiences. Those who need to hear our story will recognize themselves when we tell it. We were unable to recover from compulsive overeating by ourselves; contributing to the strength of the group is what ensures continued recovery for us all.

Sponsorship

After we have been in the OA program for a while, someone may ask us to be his or her sponsor. Even though we may feel inadequate for such a responsibility, Step Twelve suggests that we agree; sponsorship is part of carrying the message.

As sponsors, we can help new members by listening to their daily food plans, offering encouragement, and making suggestions for maintaining abstinence. We may be asked to be program sponsors, giving guidance with the Steps. Or our sponsorship may combine all elements of the program—help with physical abstinence, plus support and guidance for emotional and spiritual growth.

Honestly sharing what has happened to us and what has worked for us is our gift to make available to whoever asks for our help. In the process, we will have the satisfaction not only of making a valuable contribution but also of being more fully known and understood by someone else. We will strengthen our own abstinence and open up new directions for our personal growth in the program.

Together we can do what we cannot do alone. We all struggle with the tendency to overeat, some of us every day, many times a day. When we make suggestions to someone else, we are reminding ourselves of what we need to do in order to remain abstinent. When we know that a newcomer is looking to us for direction and guidance, we are inspired to set a good example. A phone call helps the sponsor as much as it helps the caller.

You can only share what you have. Someone chooses you as a sponsor because you have something that person wants and needs—abstinence, a measure of serenity, a well-adjusted attitude. You share the program as it works for you. The person you sponsor is free to take or reject what you give. If the relationship becomes a problem for either of you, you are each free to terminate it. In the Twelve Step programs, principles are more important than personalities.

If you do not have a sponsor, why not get one? Those of us who decide that we no longer need a sponsor's help after a certain amount of time in OA are ignoring a vital ingredient of the program. We can each profit tremendously from a continuing close relationship with someone who knows our history and has been with us through the ups and downs of our recovery.

When you have benefited from the attention of a friend and sponsor who has been helpful with your efforts to maintain abstinence and follow the Steps, you can pass along that same patient assistance to another compulsive overeater. That's the way the program works.

Practicing the Principles

Think back to the person you were when you took Step One. How have you changed? How has your life changed? To what extent have the principles of the Twelve Step program influenced your thoughts and behavior?

To "practice these principles in all our affairs" is, of course, an ideal for which we strive, knowing that we will never perfectly achieve it. Some days we feel the satisfaction of making progress. Other days we may seem to lose ground temporarily. What the program gives us is a framework for actions, decisions, and plans—a goal to aim for, even though we may miss it at times. The principles gradually become part of our personalities, and because they work, they have a marked influence on how we think and act each day.

Take honesty, for example. For most of us, the realization and admission that we were powerless over food and that our lives were a mess was the beginning of a new honesty—honesty first with ourselves and, as a result, honesty with other people.

Being honest with ourselves and our sponsor about what we are eating is a necessary ingredient of abstinence. Being honest with ourselves and the important others in our lives about our feelings and behavior is necessary for maintaining inner peace and meaningful relationships. Since we are accepted in OA just as we are, we don't need to fake anything.

From the experience of being ourselves at last, we realize the self-destructiveness of pretense and deception. We usually end up getting along much better with everyone when we stop falsifying ourselves in order to do what we think will please someone else.

Another of the principles that can profoundly affect us at a very deep level of our being is that of consciously turning over situations beyond our control—letting go and letting God. We start out by turning over our inability to control what we eat. From that beginning, we decide to relinquish more and more of our frustrations as we experience the relief and joy that come from learning to trust a Higher Power.

Turning over what we cannot handle does not mean that we do nothing, expecting God to do everything for us. We do as much as we can—for example, we write down a food plan, make telephone calls, go to meetings, search for a job if we're out of work, do our part to make relationships run smoothly, look for opportunities to be of service. We do what we can, but we trust a Higher Power to take care of the outcome.

The growing confidence we experience from turning over the unmanageable aspects of our lives and finding answers causes those around us to notice a difference. "What has happened to you? You seem very relaxed and happy." How you respond is your decision, but remember—you have been given a priceless gift. The only strings attached are that you share it.

Courage, humility, love, patience, acceptance—the continued development of these and other assets, along with continued abstinence from compulsive overeating, is contingent on our daily spiritual condition. If any one principle can be said to underlie all of the Twelve Steps, it is perhaps that of seeking and maintaining close contact with a Power greater than ourselves. If we stay in touch with the God of our understanding throughout the events of each day, we cannot go far wrong.

Practicing the principles means that we do what we need to do in order to abstain from compulsive overeating and live in harmony with ourselves and those around us. It means that we allow others to think their own thoughts, feel their own feelings, and live their own lives. It means that we are honest at home and on the job, as well as in OA meetings. It means that we do not spend a lot of time and energy worrying about whether the sky is going to fall. It means that we go out of our way to give help, because we have been helped. It means that we swallow our pride and apologize when we have made a mistake and hurt someone else. Best of all, practicing the principles of the Twelve Step program means that life takes on new direction and new joy.

Living Today

Months and years can run together and be lost in the stupor of overeating. When we take away the anesthetic of excess calories, we come alive to the realities of the present, including the sharp edges of emotions that we were trying to dull. One day at a time, we are learning to cope with the bad feelings, the good feelings, and the in-between blahs. The message that is yours and mine to share with other compulsive overeaters is that we can live each day without excess food, provided we concentrate on *today*, now, this moment.

Yes, there is life with abstinence. It is an existence filled with new sensations, new experiences, perhaps new fears, but also new hope and new faith. What was once unmanageable can be handled one day at a time with the help of the program and a Higher Power.

When you were overeating, how much time did you spend daydreaming about a fantasy future or worrying about impending disasters? Did you hash and rehash past problems? Cling to regrets and resentments? How often were you fully alert to the present moment?

With abstinence, our time and attention can be devoted to the here and now. Instead of overeating to escape anxiety about whether we will be able to pay our bills, we can use the time in productive work that will increase our income. We will never have perfect security, but we do not have to spoil today with worry about what we might not have tomorrow. The same Power that sustains us now will be with us then.

In the same way, we do not have to worry now about how hungry we might be in the morning, or tomorrow afternoon. Next week's abstinence is not our problem now. All we have to do is follow the program in the present. We are learning that we can do practically anything if it is only for twenty-four hours! We can even be courteous to the people who exasperate us if we concentrate on being polite just for today.

Sinking deeply into the present moment makes us aware of a multitude of signals that we probably missed when we were overeating. When we focus on what is happening right now, in both our inner and outer worlds, we can react appropriately to whatever comes along. Instead of planning the next binge, we can extract a maximum amount of pleasure out of the sights, sounds, feelings, and ideas that are immediately at hand. Even unpleasant situations can be a means of growth when they are faced honestly and thoughtfully.

There are many interesting and challenging things to do when we are no longer obsessed with food. We who have walked into a new life by means of OA and the Twelve Step program have been greatly blessed. Step Twelve is our ongoing way of saying thank you. Of course, the most important help we can give to other compulsive overeaters is the maintenance of our own physical, emotional, and spiritual abstinence. Beyond this, each opportunity we take to spread the good news of the program enriches our shared recovery.